THE LIBRARY OF HOLOCAUST TESTIMONIES

I Light a Candle

With best wishes

M.B.E.

The Library of Holocaust Testimonies

Editors: Antony Polonsky, Martin Gilbert CBE, Aubrey Newman, Raphael F. Scharf, Ben Helfgott MBE

Under the auspices of the Yad Vashem Committee of the Board of Deputies of British Jews and the Centre for Holocaust Studies, University of Leicester

My Lost World by Sara Rosen
From Dachau to Dunkirk by Fred Pelican
Breathe Deeply, My Son by Henry Wermuth
My Private War by Jacob Gerstenfeld-Maltiel
A Cat Called Adolf by Trude Levi
An End to Childhood by Miriam Akavia
A Child Alone by Martha Blend
The Children Accuse by Maria Hochberg-Marianska and Noe Gruss
I Light a Candle by Gena Turgel
My Heart in a Suitcase by Anne L. Fox
Memoirs from Occupied Warsaw, 1942-1945
by Helena Szereszewska
Have You Seen My Little Sister?
by Janina Fischler-Martinho
Surviving the Nazis, Exile and Siberia by Edith Sekules
Out of the Ghetto by Jack Klajman with Ed Klajman
From Thessaloniki to Auschwitz and Back
by Erika Myriam Kounio Amariglio
Translated by Theresa Sundt
I Was No. 20832 at Auschwitz by Eva Tichauer
Translated by Colette Lévy and Nicki Rensten
My Child is Back! by Ursula Pawel
Wartime Experiences in Lithuania by Rivka Lozansky Bogomolnaya
Translated by Miriam Beckerman
Who Are You, Mr Grymek? by Natan Gross
Translated by William Brand
A Life Sentence of Memories by Issy Hahn, Foreword by Theo Richmond
An Englishman in Auschwitz by Leon Greenman
For Love of Life by Leah Iglinsky-Goodman
No Place to Run: The Story of David Gilbert by Tim Shortridge and
Michael D. Frounfelter
A Little House on Mount Carmel by Alexandre Blumstein
From Germany to England Via the Kindertransports by Peter Prager
By a Twist of History: The Three Lives of a Polish Jew by Mietek Sieradzki
The Jews of Poznań by Zbigniew Pakula
Lessons in Fear by Henryk Vogler
To Live is to Forgive ... But Not Forget by Maja Abramowitch

I Light a Candle

GENA TURGEL

with Veronica Groocock

VALLENTINE MITCHELL
LONDON • PORTLAND, OR

First published in Great Britain in 1987 by Grafton Books
First published in this series in 1995 by
VALLENTINE MITCHELL
Crown House, 47 Chase Side
London N14 5BP

and in the United States of America by
VALLENTINE MITCHELL
c/o ISBS, 5824 N. E. Hassalo Street
Portland, Oregon 97213-3644

Website: www.vmbooks.com

A record of this title is with the British Library
and with the Library of Congress

ISBN 0-85303-315-3

Printed in Great Britain by Creative Print and Design (Wales),
Ebbw Vale

FRONTISPIECE: Nearly fifty years after her wedding day, the author displays the wedding dress made of British parachute silk in which she was married to Sergeant Norman Turgel in Lübeck on 6 October 1945.

Photographs 7 and 8 are reproduced by kind permission of the Imperial War Museum, London.

To the memory of my mother and
all those millions who suffered and died
at the hands of the Nazis.

Biographical Note

Gena Turgel was born in Cracow, Poland, in 1923. After the German invasion in 1939 she was confined to the ghetto, and later spent three years in concentration camps, at Plaszov, Auschwitz and Belsen. Liberated by the British Army in April 1945, she met and married Norman Turgel and moved to London later that year.

Sadly, Norman died in 1995 just two months before they would have celebrated their Golden Wedding Anniversary, showing how successful their marriage was despite knowing each other for such a short time before their wedding. Gena now lives in Stanmore, Middlesex, in close touch with their three children, eight grandchildren and two great-grandchildren.

In 2001 she was awarded the MBE for her work on the Holocaust.

Contents

List of Illustrations

The Library of Holocaust Testimonies

It is greatly to the credit of Frank Cass that this series of survivors' testimonies is being published in Britain. The need for such a series has long been apparent here, where many survivors made their homes.

Since the end of the war in 1945 the terrible events of the Nazi destruction of European Jewry have cast a pall over our time. Six million Jews were murdered within a short period; the few survivors have had to carry in their memories whatever remains of the knowledge of Jewish life in more than a dozen countries, in several thousand towns, in tens of thousands of villages, and in innumerable families. The precious gift of recollection has been the sole memorial for millions of people whose lives were suddenly and brutally cut off.

For many years, individual survivors have published their testimonies. But many more have been reluctant to do so, often because they could not believe that they would find a publisher for their efforts.

In my own work over the past two decades, I have been approached by many survivors who had set down their memories in writing, but who did not know how to have them published. I realized what a considerable emotional strain the writing down of such hellish memories had been. I also realized, as I read many dozens of such accounts, how important each account was, in its own way, in recounting aspects of the story that had not been told before, and adding to our understanding of the wide range of human suffering, struggle and aspiration.

I Light a Candle

With so many people and so many places involved, including many hundreds of camps, it was inevitable that the historians and students of the Holocaust should find it difficult at times to grasp the scale and range of the events. The publication of memoirs is therefore an indispensable part of the extension of knowledge, and of public awareness of the crimes that had been committed against a whole people.

Martin Gilbert
Merton College
Oxford

Introduction to the Second Edition

So much has happened since the first publication of this book eight years ago that I find it hard to know where to begin.

My story, the story of a survivor, is the story that six million others cannot tell. I was, and I am, and I always shall be a witness to the mass murder and systematic destruction of a civilisation.

Maybe this is my destiny. Maybe this is why I was spared, so that my testimony will serve as a memorial, like the candle that I light, to the men, women and children who have no voice.

Since my return to Belsen with the BBC in 1985, an extremely difficult and distressing experience, to say the least, and the subsequent publication of my book, Norman and I have appeared many times on national television and radio. As invited speakers, we have spoken in schools, colleges, universities, and a variety of institutions, associations and organisations far too numerous to mention. We have been interviewed and written about in newspapers and magazines.

It has not always been easy, and sometimes the emotional strain has been considerable. But if the recounting of one more experience can broaden the scope of human understanding, it is a very small price to pay.

Going back to Belsen made me appreciate even more the fact that I am alive today and able to make a small contribution to the memory of those who died.

When loss of life is on such a grand scale, it is difficult for people to see it as a tragedy. Instead it all becomes another set of statistics without a human face. To talk of the murder of six million Jews becomes almost as banal as the evil that caused it.

But these people were real. They were children and parents, uncles and aunts, doctors and teachers. They used to laugh and cry, but now they scream in silence.

We have been given the opportunity to tell a new generation, fortunate enough never to have experienced the horrors of the concentration camps, what the history books can only touch upon. If the future is to be built on the memory of the past, then it has become our duty to remind and inform the young people of today of a time, no more than half a century ago, which might otherwise be consigned to the pages of history books.

We do not speak with hatred or regret. We simply put the memory of our experience to the service of the future. It is not then confined to the past. It is there to serve as a record and as an example for the generations of today and tomorrow.

When we receive letters from schoolchildren and students telling us how little they had understood about the Holocaust until they heard us speak, we begin to realise just how powerful the telling of one actual experience really is. Sometimes it is very painful for me to remind myself about this period of my life, but it is also a great satisfaction to know that, in due course, the younger generation will be able to take their turn to 'guard the memory'.

We shall always remain grateful to Frank Cass for recognising that this book and others of its kind are not about their commercial value, and we thank him for re-publishing this book. He is a man of vision. We would also like to acknowledge the work of the Holocaust Educational Trust and the Yad Vashem Committee, to whom we are donating all our royalties.

We will continue to do our little bit for as long as we can, secure in the knowledge that they will continue to light a candle long after us.

I Light a Candle is the story of one survivor. It is also the story of all survivors. Above all, it is the story of those who were not so fortunate, and we dedicate this book to their memory.

Gena Turgel
April 1995

Acknowledgements

I would like to thank Veronica Groocock for her expert guidance in the writing of this book. It has not been easy for me to put down on paper some of the experiences which happened to myself and others, but her patience and skill have been greatly appreciated.

I would also like to thank my husband Norman who – in addition to writing one of the chapters as well as the epilogue – has been so supportive to me for so many years.

I Light a Candle

North Sea

Baltic Sea

USSR

Copenhagen

Danzig

Lübeck

Ravensbruck

Bergen/ Belsen

Treblinka

Berlin

Warsaw

Amsterdam

GREATER GERMANY

Lodz

Majdanek

Sobibor

Buchenwald

Belzec

Cracow

Prague

Plaszov

Lwow

LUXEMBOURG

Auschwitz

SLOVAKIA

GALICIA

Strasbourg

Mauthausen

Vienna

TRANSYLVANIA

Dachau

Basle

Geneva

LICHTENSTEIN

HUNGARY

Budapest

ROMANIA

Zagreb

Trieste

Venice

CROATIA

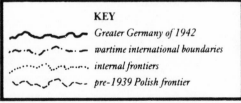

KEY

—— *Greater Germany of 1942*

·—··—· *wartime international boundaries*

········· *internal frontiers*

– – – – *pre-1939 Polish frontier*

1

We All Pray to the Same God

When I think back, I pinch myself to see if I am really alive. It seems as if I must have been made of iron to have withstood all those years of suffering. My thoughts go back to so many moments of despair, depression, terror.

I always kept, on a little shelf at the back of my mind, a feeling of determination to hold on, mainly because I was so concerned about my mother. Fighting for her existence gave me vital inner strength.

Sometimes my hopes would diminish but then, suddenly, instinctively, I felt I had to go on, I had to survive, I had to tell the world what went on.

I mourn in my own way. When I light a candle in memory of my sisters and brothers who died in the Holocaust, that is my own personal tribute. And I can never forget.

I was born on 1 February 1923, the youngest of nine children: five boys and four girls. We lived in Sarego Road in Cracow in Poland, a very select and central part of the city. Our road led to a large park in the middle of Cracow, and it was a short walk from our home to the main square.

Home was a comfortable, spacious ground-floor flat with five rooms. We had parquet floors, Persian carpets, chandeliers and good furniture. We were a respectable, affluent middle-class family, well-to-do in every sense of the word.

My parents, Samuel and Estera Goldfinger, ran a small textile business a few streets away from home. We used to buy materials from manufacturers in mill towns such as Lodz and Bielsko.

My mother was a highly capable person, liked by everyone, and she carried on the business successfully after my father died in 1932. She was a very beautiful, smartly dressed woman. A portrait of her with my father when they were engaged used to hang over the sideboard in our dining room. She looked like an elegant, aristocratic Victorian lady, with her hair pinned up and wearing a high-necked dress with padded shoulders. My father had a moustache and wore a dinner suit with a bow tie and winged collar.

He was in the Austrian Army during World War I. He had a high rank in Communications, and was stationed just outside Vienna.

Mother used to have an Alsatian dog called Rolf, who was company for her during my father's long absences. He never saw the dog until it was a few years old. Rolf always barked at strangers, but when my father walked in after being invalided out of the war, the dog jumped up and licked him, sensing that he was one of the family. This happened before I was born and was one of the stories my mother used to tell me in later years.

My memories of my father are rather hazy because he died when I was about eight years old. We had a large tiled fireplace in the dining room and he would often stand there with his back against the chimney breast, looking very distinguished.

He was ill for several years with lung trouble, as a result of his war wounds, but I am sure that Adolf Hitler's growing influence in Europe also contributed to his poor health. He died not only from his wounds but from worry and fear – the fear that Hitler would gain power in Germany and try to conquer the world. From his sickbed, where he was confined in his last year, my father could look ahead and foresee the catastrophic effect this would have on the world.

He died the year before Hitler came to power. Because of his illness, my mother was the main power in the family. She was a very courageous woman who, because she was widowed so young, directed all her ambition and drive into bringing up her children. She wanted us all to have a good education and did her best for us in that respect. When we were 14, we all went to Protestant 'evangelical' grammar schools where languages, especially French and German, were a priority.

My mother was of Austrian descent and spoke fluent German. She encouraged my brothers, sisters and me to practise German at home. This was to prove a great asset later on, in the concentration camps. The Nazis used to ask me where I had learned to speak such good German. 'Were you born in Germany?' they asked. Not many Poles knew German; it was not a compulsory subject in most schools, and so they were surprised at my command of the language.

Music and mathematics were among my best subjects at school, and I also had quite a good singing voice. We had an English tutor at home in the afternoons. We used to call him *Anglik* (Englishman). He was in his thirties and good-looking, with olive skin and dark brown hair. When he first arrived I was only about 12, but he taught some of my older sisters and brothers who by then had started at grammar school. That was when I picked up my first two English sentences: 'The sky is blue', and 'The sun is shining'.

I don't think I was a brilliant scholar, although I don't remember my schooldays very well because later events in my life completely overshadowed all recollections of those early years.

I loved the outdoor life and used to go on school outings, including mountain-climbing expeditions. After school in the winter I often went skating with my sister Miriam and friends. Our ice rink was a frozen pond. As a beginner I used to fall over so many times that my knees became cracked and bruised, but it was my favourite pastime and I enjoyed it tremendously.

Miriam and I used to play netball and table tennis together, too. We were very close. There was only one year between us and people used to regard us as twins.

On Sundays during the winter months, several of us went

skiing or tobogganing. We would climb to the top of a hill near our home, pulling our sledges, and we would ride down very fast, steering with our legs and heels. We had to muffle ourselves up well in thick scarves and bobble hats against the strong, biting wind.

Sometimes, on the flat, we rode in *kuleiki*, a row of two-seater wooden sledges tied to horses. It was great fun.

Those years of skating and *kuleiki* were the best years of my youth. What happened to me after the age of 15 more or less wiped out my adolescent years, and there was no time for boyfriends or a normal social life. In any case, girls of my generation were less mature than the girls of today. Sexual freedom did not exist and we led sheltered lives.

Ours was a traditional Jewish home and my parents were both religious but also forward-thinking. My mother was a broad-minded, modern person, and we lived in a mixed community with lots of non-Jewish friends. At Christmas she exchanged gifts with the mayor, the chief of police and other local officials and civic dignitaries, inviting them to our home for dinner.

At Easter, when we celebrate the Passover, she always invited a non-Jewish person to dinner to show them our way of life. I have heard it said that some Polish people were anti-Semitic. This may have been so in villages or rural areas, but living in a big town or city and in a mixed area one did not feel it so directly. Before the war I personally had no experience of this problem in Cracow, though historians may have a different view.

My mother was a very charitable person, always sympathetic towards those who were hungry, poor or less fortunate than ourselves. Once a year, at the Jewish festival of Purim, my father sat at the top of the table in our dining room, the front door was left wide open and all the beggars in the neighbourhood would come in and queue up at the table while my father gave them gifts of money. On their way out my mother had a parcel ready for each of them, consisting of cake, fruit and bread.

In her youth my mother used to give lessons in literacy to

people living locally who could not read or write. Some of them would come to her and ask her to compose an official letter they needed to send. This is the kind of unselfish life she led. I like to think that I may have inherited some of those characteristics from her because I do like to help people and I tend to take the side of minorities.

We always had help at home, because my mother was very busy looking after the business. A German ('evangelical') maid called Tomcia lived with us for about thirty years and had been working for my mother since my eldest brother, Herman, was in his cradle. She used to joke a lot with my brothers, and we all loved her. She was a good companion.

Mother supervised the cooking and helped prepare the meals. On Saturdays (the Jewish Sabbath) we used to eat goose or chicken, with cabbage, beans or peas.

Two of my sisters (Miriam and Hela) and I had birthdays in February, so my mother used to organise a big, combined party for us. She made a dish called *Studentenfutter*, which was a huge mixed heap of sultanas, almonds and other nuts, a popular young people's dish in Poland.

I had little in common with my older brothers and sisters, and they regarded us younger ones as almost another generation. I remember my brother, Herman, getting married. I was only about four at the time and he was more than 20 years older than me. Miriam and I were bridesmaids and wore white ballerina-style dresses trimmed with lace frills.

My second brother, Soul, was a chartered accountant and married shortly before the war.

My brother Janek was very jolly and always made us laugh, especially when he dressed up in his clown's outfit: a black and white spotted costume and pointed hat with a pompon which he made himself. He was a naturally funny man with a happy disposition, and always the centre of any party. He resembled Norman Wisdom in his mannerisms and movements.

He and another brother, Marcus, were carpet dealers, both

very capable fellows who ran their own, separate businesses. My youngest brother, Willek, was studying dentistry.

My paternal grandfather had a bakery shop. My maternal grandfather lived in a small town outside Cracow. He was a registrar and a very well-spoken, educated man, who lived to the age of 104. His father (my great-grandfather) lived to 114 – and my mother died at 99 – so we were quite a tough family.

I was only 16 when the Germans bombed our city, on 1 September 1939. For several months beforehand, we had been following the newspaper reports of Germany's invasion of Czechoslovakia and Austria, and we were all very scared. Transports kept coming in, bringing people of Jewish/Polish descent who had been evacuated to Cracow. Ever since Hitler came to power in Germany in 1933 he had been looking into people's backgrounds and ancestry. It made no difference to him if Jews belonged to a 'mixed' marriage or had assimilated into a non-Jewish culture. Many couples decided to separate, the Aryan partner staying in Germany, the Jewish partner returning to Poland.

They arrived in their thousands, carrying huge travel bags and seeking shelter from Nazi persecution. It was a sight that my mother regarded as a bad omen although, like many other Polish families, we opened our home for several months to a German couple of Jewish descent.

I remember seeing one particular Polish (non-Jewish) man who lived opposite us. He used to walk around the streets with his coat collar turned up and his hat pulled down over his forehead. His eyes were wild, like a frightened animal. People in the neighbourhood said that he had been in a concentration camp, but no one knew for certain what had happened to him, where and why. He must have been a political prisoner.

Mother may have known more about him but judged it better not to tell us children. The man looked thoroughly worn, as though he had been through some terrible experience. It was the first time that I had heard anything about a concentration camp.

People began stocking up their larders with extra provisions, in readiness for the possible outbreak of hostilities. Having already lived through one world war, my mother knew the kind of supplies one required in wartime and she bought up sacks of potatoes, flour and butter, and kept them in the cellar.

She told us about the time she sent food parcels to my father when he was in the Austrian Army. To us children, the idea of war seemed very strange, almost unreal. I remember seeing film trailers in our local cinema, about the Germans and their 'achievements' – the different places they had already occupied. Still photographs illustrating this were on display in the showcase outside. This was a few days before the Germans invaded Poland.

We never fully believed that this would (or could) happen to us, and when it did we were unprepared and shocked. First, we heard a single aeroplane slowly circling in the sky over our house, just one plane flying very low. We thought it was the Polish Army on manoeuvres, and yet the sound of the engine was so different from our own aircraft – deeper and more sinister.

Then, when I walked out into the street and glanced up at the sky, I saw several planes, all flying low, all bearing the black-and-white German insignia on their sides.

There was panic among our people, with everyone running this way and that. When the bombing started a few hours later, we all ran to the shelter across the street. It was absolutely terrifying and sounded as if the whole of Cracow was being flattened. We learned later that it was mainly the outskirts that had been hit and the city itself was relatively unscathed.

The bombing went on for two days and stopped about five a.m. on Sunday, 3 September. Then there was silence. After two or three hours, the German Army marched into Cracow. A full military band accompanied the soldiers as they walked through the city streets. The young boys of the Hitler Youth, blond and neat in their uniforms, strode out in front like mascots.

It was a dry, sunny autumn morning. The windows of our flat faced the main street and we could see the proud, arrogant way the men were marching. People in the neighbourhood were peering out at the scene from behind their curtains, too frightened to go outside to see exactly what was happening.

The agony started on that day. Everything stopped, public buildings were shut down, food was rationed, Jewish people's homes were requisitioned and the occupants thrown out on to the street.

The porter in our block of flats took possession of the most exclusive apartment and evicted the Jewish occupants, who had nowhere else to go. This became common practice throughout Cracow, with porters and maids taking over their employers' property (if the Nazis hadn't beaten them to it).

There was a bank on the corner of our street and some Germans stopped outside and immediately took possession of it. They took over shops, schools, newspapers, radio stations, government institutions, all the important buildings in the city.

Before the war the political situation in Poland was very complex, with a broad spectrum of parties and factions. There were four main political movements: Socialists, Nationalists, Peasants, and Christian Democrats. Each was strongly represented in Parliament, and Polish Jews voted in the same manner as their non-Jewish counterparts. There were also 'fringe' groups: on the right, the Fascist Falanga (Phalanx), and on the left, the Communist KPP, an offshoot of the Socialists.

They censored the Press to the extent that we were left with only one newspaper, which appeared at lunchtime. It contained a little bit of truth and a little bit of propaganda, and we all had to learn to read between the lines.

First of all, we gathered around our radio set at home listening to the news broadcasts from London. We were so relieved when, two days after seeing that solitary plane above Cracow, we heard that our Allies, England and France, had declared war on Germany and that we were no longer on our own. But the fear of the future – of the Unknown – was very great.

Most of the men had been called up to the Polish Army,

including my brother Janek who left behind a wife (Fridka) and four-year-old son (Sami). We completely lost trace of Herman and Soul for some time. There was no means of communication and it was as if the whole world had been cut away.

Before the Germans invaded, hundreds of people had packed their things and started walking, trying to get out of Poland. Some, among them my brother Soul, got as far as the Russian border.

He told me when we were reunited years later that he had been captured by the Russians at Lwow (Lemberg) and taken across the border into the Soviet Union. He was sent to a work camp in a village surrounded by woods and remained there until 1945, working in an office as a chartered accountant. The camp had none of the restrictions of concentration camps, and he and his wife were well treated, not tortured or abused. After the war he was allowed back into Poland, and from there he emigrated to Israel.

Everybody tried to find some form of transport to escape – a car, or horse and wagon – but sooner or later cars were requisitioned by the Nazis, or they simply ran out of petrol, and it was common to see vehicles scattered and abandoned on the city streets.

There were six of us at home: Mother, three sisters (Miriam, Hela and my oldest sister, Sala), one brother (Willek) and myself.

My family had relations in Chicago. My mother's cousin, Dr Thorek, was an eminent doctor there, and we had planned to leave Poland and stay with him, but we left it too late. The Germans quickly closed all exit and entry points, and we could go nowhere.

A few hours before they invaded, my mother advised me to put on old clothes and make myself look less attractive. Rumours were spreading that the German soldiers were planning to rape the women, and she was terrified that this might happen to us. Luckily, we found out that it was a capital offence for them to fraternise with Jewish girls and women, because of the *Rassen-*

schande (race shame) – Hitler's obsession with Aryan purity, his belief in the Master Race. And so we were spared.

After a few weeks, all sorts of restrictions were introduced. Jews were banned from trains and trams. We had to wear the Star of David at all times, a blue star on a white band which had to be 'pure' white. The slightest blemish could mean that the wearer might be shot.

Jewish people no longer had rights. Even when we walked in the street, if we saw a German approaching we had to step off the pavement into the road to let him pass. Sometimes, this could be very dangerous and we could have got run over, but if we disobeyed they would have no hesitation in hitting us. '*Weg! Weg!*' ('Away! Away!') they shouted. They acted with such superiority, as if to emphasise: 'We are *It*. We are the Führer's children.'

By now there were posters all over the city stipulating that no Jewish family had the right to employ a maid and that all maids, therefore, must leave Jewish households. My mother begged Tomcia to go, because her life as well as ours would have been at stake had she continued to work for us. We helped her pack her bags, but she didn't want to leave us. In our own interests – and hers – we had to persuade her to go.

Someone came to collect her and we all felt very sad when we parted. We were crying and she was crying, because she knew that for Jewish people the future was not a bright one. She went back to her family in Germany and we never heard anything of her again.

By this time, our couple of Jewish/German evacuees had also moved on.

Herman, my eldest brother, ran a small jewellery shop and lived with his family in a town called Tarnow, a three-hour train journey from Cracow. Sala and I went to see him there soon after war broke out, but several months later, when we were in the ghetto, we heard that he was dead. Friends who lived in the same town told us that the Nazis had entered his room with machine-guns and shot him down, along with his wife and their three children.

After a few months at the Front, all Jewish soldiers were segregated by the Germans into separate barracks, then ordered on to a special truck which was bound for a POW camp. On his way there, Janek managed to roll down the side of the train and escape. In the middle of the night we heard a knock at our front door – and there he was.

His wife and son had been staying with us while he was away. Janek arrived looking unshaven and exhausted after spending many days at the Front. He had also walked many miles after escaping from the train. Mother was relieved and at the same time frightened at his haggard appearance.

Around this time there were posters on display, telling all Jewish people to register for an identity card, which had to be stamped. We had to go to a big hall, part of a State building which the Nazis had occupied. Inside, there was a long flight of stairs, with people going up one side and coming down the other.

In the big hall upstairs, various SS clerks sat behind tables and asked us questions: 'Where were you born? . . . What are you doing here?' We had to attend in alphabetical order: surnames A to G on one day, H to M on another day, and so on.

Every morning we had to assemble outside a building designated by the Nazis as the 'Labour Exchange', where we were allocated jobs. Groups of us were taken in trucks to do whatever work was needed: unloading supplies from planes at the airport; picking potatoes in the fields; unloading transports of coal from goods trains on to trucks.

Sometimes, even before we registered, lorries used to stop in the street and Jewish people were picked up at random to do various jobs in the city: mostly manual work like cleaning windows, scrubbing floors, shovelling coal. This happened to me several times. I remember once climbing a ladder to clean some windows and cutting myself on the glass quite badly.

The Germans continued to take over people's homes and throw

them out on to the street. They sent some of us to go in and clean up the houses and flats prior to their reoccupation. Among other tasks, we had to fill large buckets with coal and carry them into the cellars.

All the time the guards were whipping us and rushing us, *'Schnell! Schnell!'* I was young and physically fit, but it was back-breaking work and not the kind to which I was accustomed. The shovels they gave us were very heavy, but we didn't think of the pain or how exhausted we felt. Somehow we had to find the strength to carry on. We were aware of the guards standing there watching, their fingers poised on the triggers of their rifles. How shaky we felt and how fast we had to work.

In those early months there were constant reminders of our oppression: swastikas painted on the sides of buildings, hostile signs all over the city: 'Jews are not wanted', 'Jews must be murdered', 'Jews are scum'.

We used to witness such horrifying sights. One day I heard the sound of chains clanking outside in the street. I ran out and saw a group of about thirty men chained to each other by the feet and hands, several rows deep, dragging and shuffling themselves along. They were the mill owners from Lodz, a manufacturing town similar in size and type to Bradford in the north of England.

These were well respected and distinguished people, and they were being made to walk all through Poland. When I saw them, they were almost unrecognisable. They looked filthy, unshaven, starving and ill, like slaves in a chain gang.

You could tell how many weeks they must have been travelling already, from their dishevelled, pathetic appearance – their torn, shabby clothes, the scars on their backs, hands and faces. They held placards in front of them with the words: 'We Are the War Mongers'.

I don't know how much longer they could have held out, as they looked in such poor physical condition. They were closely guarded by the SS with Alsatian dogs, and so we were unable to give them any food or drink. People were too frightened even to look at such scenes, let alone to act.

The shock we received from incidents like these was impossible to describe.

On another occasion, I was walking with Sala when we noticed a young Jewish fellow with a long beard coming along towards us. A jeep stopped nearby and a Nazi official stepped out. I remember thinking: 'My goodness, I hope they are not coming to *us*.'

The Nazi walked towards the Jewish man. '*Halt!*' he cried, and called him over. He then produced a pair of scissors from his pocket and went 'snip snip' at the man's beard – and in the process he sliced some of the man's flesh away. Blood poured down into pools on the pavement. The Nazi gave the man several sharp kicks in the groin and the man lay groaning on the ground. We ran away, terrified and deeply distressed.

That night, Sala was so frightened that she said she was going away, she didn't care where. She joined another group of people and they left. I lost trace of her until after the war, when I heard that she had ended up in a concentration camp in Germany. (She survived and now lives in Israel.)

The kind of incident which I have just described was a regular occurrence. Some Jewish men used to walk along hiding their beards inside their coats. Hitler's aim was to destroy the Jewish faith and any other religion that failed to conform to Nazi ideology.

Today, we live in a world where some people wear turbans, Indian women wear saris, Arabs have their prayer mats. Everyone should be free to express their religion openly and without fear. I can be friendly with a nun, a priest or a rabbi. We all pray to the same God in different ways.

2

A Change in Priorities

From the moment the Germans entered our city, we had to fight for our lives. I had to forget my dreams of being a doctor. I had always wanted to study medicine, but there was no time for any teacher to advise me, no time to discuss the possibilities open to me.

In the first week of the war, Jewish and Polish schools and colleges were closed down, and the Germans began commandeering all Jewish businesses. Some of the goods they seized were transported to Germany. They took sewing machines, radios, silver, whatever they could get their hands on. Jewish people had forfeited the right to run or own a business.

Polish shops and businesses continued to run normally, but I do not recall whether Polish (non-Jewish) schools and colleges were gradually reopened. We were too preoccupied with our own troubles, and with the daily struggle for survival under Nazi rule, to notice what was happening to others elsewhere.

This is what occurred in relation to our own business. My brother Willek was looking after the flat belonging to Soul and his wife, who had left their home in Cracow and found themselves in Russian-occupied Poland. As a safeguard against the flat being requisitioned Willek slept there.

Soul had a maid, a Polish woman of German descent, who had a spare set of keys to the flat. She wanted the flat for herself and resented the idea of Willek staying there, so she went to the SS headquarters in the main square and informed them that this man was sleeping in the flat which belonged to his brother.

One evening, when Willek was about to enter the flat, three SS men in civilian clothes approached him, pointing a gun at his head and warning him that he was under arrest unless he gave up the keys to where he lived. They were Gestapo, and later on they brought him over to us. It was around midnight. My mother was fast asleep and she woke up to see these three tall men in black leather coats and brandishing guns, standing over her bed.

'What is it? What's going on?' she said. They said to her: 'Your son will be shot now, in front of you, unless you take back everything which you've removed from the other flat.'

My mother told them she had taken nothing but they were obviously just looking for an excuse to harass us. We suspected that it was Soul's maid, a nasty, two-faced woman, who had been stealing things from their flat.

'You can look – I have my own belongings,' Mother told the men.

'In that case,' they said, 'we will take all that you have.'

They opened the wardrobe and pulled out the contents into a heap on the floor. My mother was very fond of linen and had some lovely items of the finest quality. The Germans went around our flat callously picking out things they wanted. They said: 'We'll have this . . . and this . . . and that,' and they gave us orders to deliver them all, together with the keys from the business, to the SS headquarters in the main square by noon the following day.

By now, we had all moved into the living room. My mother was still in her nightdress and dressing gown and the men were rummaging through our belongings when the front door suddenly opened and in came my brother Marcus. He had spent the evening with friends in the neighbourhood after work, and he wandered casually in, completely unaware of what was going on but immediately jumping to the wrong conclusions. He challenged the men: 'Who are you? Show me your identification.' Rumours had been circulating that a number of bogus SS were going about openly robbing people in their homes by dressing up in black leather clothes and posing as Gestapo agents.

The three men identified themselves to Marcus but this was his first experience of coming face to face with the SS, and so he was naturally suspicious and felt justified in questioning them.

All the time I was pinching him, trying to get the message across to him that these were genuine Gestapo and had already shown us their identity cards. 'Leave it alone,' I whispered to him.

The men were getting really angry by this time. They wanted to know who this person was who had interrupted them so rudely. They disliked his attitude, and one of them was starting to reach for his gun. We were all in a state of shock, trembling and pleading with them, 'Please don't shoot him!'

My sister Hela told them: 'Oh, he doesn't know what he is talking about.' She was trying to pretend that Marcus was a bit simple-minded and therefore not responsible for his actions. Then she opened the living room door and pushed him into a corridor which led to the kitchen. We'd never had a key for this door, but, by a sheer coincidence, Willek found a spare key in his pocket and it just happened to fit the door, so he quickly locked it behind Marcus and pocketed the key again.

The man who had drawn his pistol turned to us and said: 'He was lucky, because I was going to shoot him.'

After they had gone, Marcus crept back into the room and Mother said to him: 'You had better disappear. Take some clothes and get away from here – fast.' We were frightened that those men would send somebody else to arrest Marcus, and he left immediately and went to stay with some people he knew on the other side of town. He then marched off somewhere, was eventually arrested and spent some time in a concentration camp in Germany (a different one from our sister Sala's). We did not see each other again until after the war, when we were both living in London.

Meanwhile, Soul's maid moved into their flat. We would be

left with the barest of necessities: wardrobes, beds, bedding, a table. We felt a mixture of fear and sadness: the fear that they might shoot us all, and sadness at the ruthless searching of our home, the prospect of losing nearly everything we owned.

The following morning, we had to hire a horse and wagon – at our own expense. We gathered up all our precious possessions and stacked them on the back of the wagon: linen, lampshades, silver candlesticks, trays . . . and the keys from the business.

We took the horse and wagon to the SS headquarters in the central square, now renamed Adolf Hitler Platz. It was a very attractive part of Cracow, with flower sellers, an arcade of shops, a beautiful Catholic church, and a weekly market where farmers came to sell their produce of butter, eggs, fruit.

We unloaded the wagon, which took some time, then returned it to the hiring company.

Later that day, one of the Gestapo returned to our home to check whether we had delivered every item they had specified on their 'itinerary'. He walked into one of the bedrooms and noticed a long handle sticking out from the top of the wardrobe – the handle of a tennis racket. We were scared at this apparent oversight and said: 'Oh, we forgot about that.' He made us reach up and lift the racket down from the wardrobe, then he called in his driver, who took it away.

After the raid on our home, my mother was speechless. She tried hard not to show us how much she was suffering, but we lived under an enormous strain all the time. Our business was finished. The Germans must have taken all the cloth and sold it. They probably transported the sewing machines to Germany.

My mother had pinned a note on our front door saying that she was the widow of an Austrian Army invalid, hoping this would make the Nazis leave her alone. But even after the raid, they still kept coming every few days and pestering her, along with the other Jewish people in our block. About half the residents were Jewish.

Some Polish people collaborated with the Nazis but, equally,

there were others who helped the Jews, and members of my own
family experienced the support of several Polish families. As I
shall relate later, Janek went into hiding with Polish friends
outside the ghetto. Their lives could have been in danger if they
had been discovered harbouring a Jew, and they took a big risk.

These regular visits from the Gestapo went on for several
weeks. There were different men, and not all of them knew that
our home had already been ransacked. They used to rap loudly
on the door, demanding to know who lived there and nosing
around the place to see what they could scrounge. There was no
hesitation: if they wanted something, they just helped themselves.

In their black leather coats, with their whips and their big boots,
they looked so sure of themselves, so arrogant, as if to say: 'We
are the ones who dictate the terms. You are nothing.'

After a few weeks our priorities changed, and we began to come
to terms with our loss. We may have sacrificed our possessions, but
we still had our lives and our self-respect. We no longer attached
too much importance to material objects.

Mentally, however, we were all affected in different ways.
Willek was now 20, four years older than me, and very tall, but
whenever we went out together he was so terrified of the SS that
he clung to me, hiding behind me like a child sheltering beneath
his mother's skirts. The tremendous shock of being held at
gunpoint by the Gestapo in Soul's flat had shattered his nerves,
and he never fully recovered from the experience.

He stayed with us for a while, but after we were sent to the
ghetto he moved in with his Jewish girlfriend, Nusia, who was
studying to be a nursery teacher.

Shortly after the Gestapo 'break-in', we received an unexpected
visit from a mill owner and former client of ours, a man called
Bartelmus. He arrived in full Nazi uniform and wanted to know
if we still had some material which we could give him. He was
surprised when we told him that he was too late because every
last remnant had been removed.

We were trembling, astonished to discover that he had turned out to be one of *them.* We had never dreamed that a man of his calibre would have associations with the SS. However, he lived in the mill town of Bielsko, where many of the inhabitants were of German descent, a fact which they exploited, preferring to highlight the German side of their heritage.

A couple of months after they invaded, the Germans began stepping up their activities. They began segregating people, sending them away on transports to concentration camps. They wasted no time. Their organisation was meticulous. Everything had to be done to the letter.

Sometimes they didn't even bother with 'official' segregations. They just called at people's homes, sent them away in a truck to the woods and shot them. They would take old people in groups of ten, hundreds of them, from many of the small towns and villages around Cracow. After they had rounded up the people and shot them, the Germans grabbed their belongings for themselves.

One elderly couple, whose name was Klan, died in this way. They were neighbours of ours and they moved in with their son and his wife. Because the son's wife was non-Jewish, they thought they would be safe, but the Nazis located them and packed them into a truck with some other elderly people. They never came back.

The Nazis used sadistic methods. They might say to the people: 'Bring some clothes, a few belongings: you are going to another town'; or 'You are going to see your daughter/aunt/nephew', or 'You are being taken to an *Arbeitslager* [labour camp]: it will be paradise.'

On Hitler's birthday, 20 April, everyone had to deliver all their valuables to the SS headquarters. Families parted with mountains of copper, steel and silver. Anything made of metal had to go. All we had left to give were some brass spoons and a coffee grinder.

We were forbidden to keep any item with fur on it, not even any trimmings. I had to remove the Persian fur collar from my charcoal grey coat and hand it over to the Nazis.

Mother, anticipating the raid on our home, had given some of her best clothes, including a fur coat, to Polish friends for safekeeping. Whenever she wanted a particular item, she would go to them and collect it. If, in the meantime, these people wished to buy any of them, they gave Mother some money which was less than the true value – maybe only a third of the original price – but it helped us to get by.

Once, when she went to claim a particular item from them, they denied all knowledge of it. 'No, you didn't give it to us,' they said. This was our first direct experience of anti-Semitism.

My sister Hela knew someone with an interest in Persian carpets, and we had left a carpet with these same people. She managed to get it back, and she sold it. She heard of others who had items they wanted to sell, and so she acted as an agent, earning commission. People were coming in from other towns and Hela used to barter with them, exchanging goods that they were interested in buying.

We were faced with many restrictions in our lives, but out of every misfortune comes a ray of hope. Opposite our flat lived an old schoolfriend of my mother's, and her daughter who worked at the Nazis' HQ. This woman was German but of Polish descent, and she felt very sorry for my mother when she learned that we had lost most of our possessions along with our livelihood. My mother was always handy with her needle and she altered a blouse for her friend's daughter. In return, the woman gave us some flour, sugar and other (extra) provisions which we needed.

Her daughter had a friend called Ursula Mauf, who worked as a clerk in the office of a bicycle shop. She was about 21, an attractive, cultured girl who had trained to be a ballet dancer. We became friends and I told her about the night the Gestapo broke into our home.

She was sympathetic. 'How do you manage to live?' she asked me. I said that it was very difficult and that we were on the point of starvation, so she offered to help us. She gave me her ration book and some money, and I used to shop regularly for her.

She let me keep almost everything that I purchased: packets of sugar, cooking oil, coffee, flour. She must have taken pity on us, and so she trusted me, as such actions could have got us both into serious trouble.

One day Ursula said that she had a bicycle to sell. In Poland at that time a bicycle was considered a very special item and was in great demand. Most cars had been requisitioned by the Nazis, and train services were extremely limited. German-manufactured bikes were the most reliable and convenient means of transport, but they were in short supply and only obtainable on the black market or through personal contacts. I became a kind of agent or go-between in a small, unofficial bicycle business.

About four people were involved in each transaction, and we arranged by telephone that I would fetch a bicycle and hand it over to a 'middle-man'. The bicycle showroom was in the main square, a part of the city which was now out of bounds to Jewish people. Fortunately, my fair skin and blond hair made it easy for me to pass as non-Jewish, and so I took a chance. I used to walk along with a mackintosh slung over my arm so that it covered the blue and white 'Star of David' band. I prayed that no one would stop and question me.

The showroom was situated on the near side of the square, with the Catholic church on the right hand side. Opposite the church was the Nazi HQ.

We met in a little turning just off the square. It was usually a different fellow each time who came with the money. We guessed each other's identity by a pre-arranged signal: a folded newspaper under the arm, a certain colour tie or coat. We said 'Good morning', he gave me the money, and then I went into the square, turned right and walked a few yards to the showroom where Ursula was waiting for me with the bike. Without exchanging more than a few words, I gave her the money, took the bike, wheeled it around the corner and into the turning, gave it to the fellow and quickly left the scene.

I never met the actual buyer, but it was the same procedure and the same source each time. I would telephone to say that I had a bicycle and ask if someone could come and collect it. I told them the price, time and place.

We usually met around lunchtime, when not many people were in the area, and always in that turning.

It was a brief personal transaction – 'one-two-three' and away. All the time I was shaking with tension and trying not to think about the eyes that might be watching me from the Nazi HQ across the square. I could have been in grave danger. The buyer, for all I knew, might have had connections with the SS and sent somebody to arrest me. If my mackintosh had slipped off my arm and someone had seen my Star of David band, I would probably have been dragged off to the Nazi HQ and tortured. I'd heard stories of how they used to hang people upside down and interrogate them as a prelude to shooting them.

The 'commission' I earned (via Ursula) from each transaction was enough to feed us all for a couple of weeks, and was a big help to us in our straitened circumstances. I felt proud of being able to contribute to the family budget in this way.

But soon, once again, there were huge posters plastered all over the city, urging all those who had not yet obtained a stamp on their card to register immediately. These people were then sent away on transports to concentration camps. Those who, like us, had already had our cards stamped, were allowed to stay put for the time being.

A few months later we were told to register for another stamp, and the ones who obtained the stamp were ordered into the ghetto, while those without it were evacuated to Borek, a village about 30 kilometres outside Cracow. None of our family managed to acquire a stamp on this occasion, as the quota of vacant accommodation in the ghetto had been fully allocated.

So, along with hundreds of other Jewish Poles, we left Cracow for Borek. We hired a horse and wagon, and Mother travelled on the wagon, together with our few remaining possessions.

When we reached Borek we had to look for rented accommodation. From our nice comfortable home in the centre of the city,

Mother, Hela, Miriam, Willek and I found ourselves squashed into a very small room in a large block of flats. The room was sparsely furnished, with two beds, a studio couch and, in one corner, a coal-fired stove.

Food was very scarce, especially meat, but thanks to Ursula Mauf's ration book we were able to barter with the local farmers, trading in scarce commodities such as a bottle of vodka for sausages, eggs, butter. In Poland at that time a bottle of vodka was like an ounce of gold and very strong, with about 95 per cent alcohol content.

Whatever we had we saved, or exchanged for something else that we needed more. In the summer of 1940 we bought apples and other fruit from the farmers, but the winter was very tough. We used to go to the woods nearby and bring back some logs for the fire. We were almost destitute.

We lived a communal life together, each of us contributing in whatever way we could to the family kitty. My mother practised her needlework skills, doing alterations for some people we knew who were staying near us. I telephoned Ursula to ask if she had any more bicycles to sell, and whenever she succeeded in getting one, I would notify the buyer by telephone in the usual way and we organised a sale. I did this less frequently than before because of the extra complications – and risks – involved in travelling to Cracow.

It was a long, cold bus ride from Borek to Cracow. It was November when I resumed the bicycle transactions, and the seats on the bus were icy-cold. When I tried to get up at the end of the journey, I found that my coat had stuck to the seat. I was frozen through.

I can remember sitting on the bus with my raincoat draped over my arm so that it concealed the Star of David. I was shaking from the cold – and from fear that somebody might recognise me or guess that I was Jewish. Buses and trams were, of course, no-go areas for Jewish people.

I used to keep these trips a secret from my mother, otherwise she might have panicked, worrying about my safety. I had kept her informed about them while we were still living at home in Cracow, but after we moved to Borek the dangers involved were much greater.

Mother was always very anxious until I returned from one of these 'business' outings. 'Where have you been? Why were you so long?' she would ask, so relieved to see me back again.

On the way from Cracow, I used Ursula's ration book to buy some provisions – flour, rice, sugar – to bring the family.

We tried to do our best from Borek, but it was very difficult and we lost track of what was happening outside. The Nazis were still in control in the city, but Borek was far enough away for them not to come and bother us.

We were there for almost a year, then another batch of posters appeared, informing us that on such-and-such a day we had to move into the ghetto. Thousands of Jewish people were being sent away on transports from the ghetto, a mass exodus making space for the rest of us, the Jews in Borek, to take their places.

So, once again, we had to adjust to living under the constant scrutiny of the Nazis but with the added rigours of ghetto life to contend with. For us, it was another step down. Maybe even ten steps down.

3

In the Ghetto

Each major Polish city had a ghetto. Many of these dated almost from the beginning of the war. Some were based in Jewish areas; others, like the Cracow ghetto, were in non-Jewish areas.

It was autumn 1941 when we moved into the ghetto in Cracow. We walked from Borek back to Cracow, carrying a sack of potatoes, some flour and a few other belongings. First, we were taken to a place where we were allocated accommodation. We were crammed into a dark ten-by-eight ground-floor room which looked on to a courtyard. There were five of us: Mother, Willek, Hela, Miriam and me. We had to share a kitchen and bathroom with two other families, one next door and the other family in a room across the corridor.

It was a very hard winter and we slept in our thickest clothes. There was a fireplace in one corner of the room, but coal was very scarce and the nights were so frosty that our bedding literally froze to the wall and we had to wrench it away, afraid of tearing it in the process.

Some people we knew lived in even worse conditions so we didn't grumble. We were thankful just to be alive, though we began to worry a lot about the future. With the tall, iron-barred gates locked behind us, we felt completely hemmed in, with no means of escape.

The ghetto was situated on the outskirts of the city on the other side of the river, in a suburb called Podgüze. A bridge separated the area from the city centre. Each of the main gates had two openings, one for pedestrians, the other for vehicles, and was guarded on both sides by Nazis and Polish *kapos* (police).

No one was allowed to leave the ghetto without a pass – and a very special reason, such as the purchase of some medicines from a particular chemist's shop.

Life was tough. Food prices were high because of severe shortages. Goods had to be smuggled in, and we had to barter to survive.

As Jews were no longer in a position to marry, many of them went through a civil 'betrothal' ceremony in which a rabbi came and blessed the couple. My sister Miriam had a boyfriend who was an architect, a few years older than her. He was very good to us and often used to bring us some bread. They were very much in love and he asked Mother if they could get married. At that stage, young people didn't look too far ahead. They wanted to pair up and enjoy a little brief happiness, even if it was only two days or two weeks.

Mother agreed and she organised a 'wedding', inviting a rabbi to give the blessing. This took place in our room, and afterwards Miriam and her 'husband' Henek moved in with his parents, partitioning off their kitchen to make an extra room.

My brother Janek lived a few streets away with his wife Fridka and their son Sami, a beautiful blond child of about three. One day Janek was on his way to visit us when a man walked over to him and asked his name and address. Janek told him.

This man, a non-Jewish Pole, was dangerous because he was acting as an informer for the Nazis. His name was Spitzler and everybody knew about him. He used to wander around the streets in civilian clothes, looking for 'material' to deliver to his superiors in order to gain privileges. He was a tall, dark man with a hard, cynical expression. He stared at you and took your name, and before you knew it you were likely to find yourself on the next transport to a concentration camp.

When he reached our room, Janek told us what had happened.

Mother was very concerned and said she hoped that Mr Spitzler would not take action against Janek.

The following morning Janek received a letter telling him to report to Nazi headquarters later that day. Sensing that they might send him away, he managed to get himself a pass. One stood a good chance of getting a pass if a few coins were slipped into the hands of a Polish policeman, and Janek was a friendly fellow with a pleasant way about him. He left the ghetto to hide with a Polish family he knew in the city.

When he failed to appear at HQ, a Gestapo agent and a Jewish *kapo* came in the middle of the night with their rifles and knocked loudly on my sister-in-law's door. 'Where is your husband?' they asked. She told them she didn't know, but they refused to believe her, and hit her several times.

Then they took her and the little boy and came round to us. They banged and yelled, 'Open the door!'

'Who's there?' asked my mother. 'This is the police,' they said, and they burst in, brandishing their guns.

I was shaking like a leaf. 'Where is your son?' they asked. We said we didn't know, and they took Janek's wife to the police station to question her. The boy remained with us.

About six o'clock the following morning, Hela and I went with our little nephew to the police station, hoping to see some sign of Janek's wife. Hundreds of other people were waiting for their relatives, too. We saw women coming out of the building and being pushed like cattle on to a big open truck parked outside. We were some distance away, peeping out from a narrow turning across the road. We watched the truck move away.

We then noticed, slightly further away, a second, stationary truck filling up with women. Loads of women, all standing. Suddenly we saw my sister-in-law climbing into the truck. We were terribly upset at this but then, suddenly, the guards started shouting, ordering the women down from the truck. They released them all and my sister-in-law rushed over to us and took the little boy in her arms. We were so relieved.

The administration of the ghetto was run by the Jewish police. It was they who allocated the work, and they were answerable to the German and Polish police. One heard on the grapevine the best, most desirable places to work, and one of them was the uniforms factory. It used to be a chocolate factory (run by a firm called Optima) until the Nazis requisitioned it and turned it into one of their many ventures for the German war effort. My mother, Hela and I managed to get work there. Although the conditions were far from ideal, at least we were under a roof and not working outside in the fields, as many Jewish people were. Such work was infinitely preferable to scrubbing floors and lavatories, cleaning windows and the other laborious jobs to which we had often been relegated.

We worked alternate day and night shifts. On the day shift we worked from seven in the morning until late at night, with hardly a break and for no wages.

It was an enormous building with several floors and row upon row of machines on each one. It was very noisy, overcrowded and stuffy.

At first we were working on the old uniforms, which were made of a coarse, heavy cloth. They were reversible green and white duffel coats and trousers: the green acted as a camouflage against the trees in summer; the white toned in with the snow in winter.

They were dirty and infested with huge lice, and I often had to run out to the cloakroom, itching, and strip down to my underwear, shaking off the insects from my clothes, skin and hair. My hair was very long, down to my hips.

My mother was working on the other side of the room, next to the window. We were both doing the same kind of work: undoing seams, cleaning and patching up the uniforms.

It was such unpleasant, irksome work that everybody tried to transfer to the new uniforms when the material for these arrived several weeks later. We were among the lucky ones. The new material was lighter, much easier to handle and, of course, more hygienic. It was good to be away from those lice.

Each floor was supervised by a Jewish foreman, but now and again a party of Nazis would turn up and we all had to stand to attention while they walked by and inspected our work.

While I was at the factory I caught pneumonia and was off work for several weeks. During that time Miriam covered for me. One needed to be a diplomat as well as a slave. Work was a kind of status symbol. It was very important to be seen to be working, as the Nazis were meticulous with their lists and if they found out that someone was absent from their place of work, that person was regarded as worthless, a candidate for destruction.

So each morning Miriam clocked in for me, reporting for work on my behalf before going on to her own job outside the ghetto. She was secretary to a group of architects supervised by her 'husband' Henek, and they were based in the main square of the city.

The doctors could do little to cure pneumonia in those days, as there were no antibiotics, but I recovered slowly thanks to an old-fashioned remedy involving a spirit lamp. You heat it up and it helps to draw out the impurities from the body. First, you take a small blown glass and put a little spirit (alcohol) in a dish. Then you dip some cotton wool in the spirit and wipe it around the inside of the glass. Finally, you place the glass over a lighted candle, then straight on to the body.

My brother Janek was still in hiding outside the ghetto. He was never long in one place and had to move on constantly, but he sent messages to us whenever he could. Sometimes he would telephone, but he had to be careful to alter his voice and name to avoid detection by the SS – in case the lines were bugged. The telephone was in an office a few doors away from where we lived.

Janek stayed away for two months. In the meantime, more posters appeared instructing us to register. With every registration came more segregations, more transports swallowing up old people, young people and children, taking them to concentration camps in Poland and Germany.

We had little idea of how the war was progressing, as newspapers were heavily censored and few people had access to radios. Any news came to us by word of mouth – gossip or rumour.

Life in the ghetto was unreal, and people's main preoccupation concerned the date of the next transport . . . would it be *their* turn next? We lived from day to day and kept hoping the war would end soon.

We sent word to Janek that he must come and register. If he failed to show up he would be ineligible to obtain a pass or any rations in the future. However, we were worried about how he would manage to register safely without being recognised. Mr Spitzler was still on the prowl, looking for trouble, searching every street and checking on people whom he could present to the officials in return for some personal reward or favour.

Janek decided to disguise himself. He bandaged his head over one eye so that one side of his face was completely covered. He waited in the queue in front of me, with this enormous bandage tied round his chin while Spitzler walked up and down the hall staring malevolently at people. My heart was pounding. Thank goodness he didn't recognise Janek, who was trying to avoid catching Spitzler's eye. He showed his card, got a stamp and left.

Mother and I both had our cards stamped and we were dismissed, but we could see other people being segregated to other doors, other areas.

Every segregation, for us, was a miraculous achievement. It was as if we had sunk to rock bottom and surfaced again.

After Janek had his card stamped, he hid indoors with a family outside the ghetto and did not dare go out for a while. Later we heard rumours that Spitzler had been sent elsewhere. He had served his purpose, at least for the time being, so Janek returned to the ghetto.

Then came another segregation followed by another transport, this time involving women and children. We lined up in twos along the street. I stood next to my mother; in front of us were my sister-in-law and her child. At the head of the queue a Nazi and a Jewish *kapo* were standing, segregating people. They told my sister-in-law and her son to join the group on our right, and my mother and myself went to the left.

When I turned round I could see the women and children in the other group already marching off. I waited until the guards were looking the other way and then waved to my sister-in-law, indicating that she should let the boy come with *us*. He rushed over towards us, but when he was only a couple of feet away, the Jewish *kapo* noticed and said: 'No – he must go *here*, with the mother.' He was showing off, trying to assert his authority in front of the Nazi, and the two men dragged the child screaming and yelling away from us and back to his mother.

We had heard that this was to be the first transport from the ghetto to Auschwitz. They marched away and we never saw or heard from them again.

Whether or not we could have saved that little boy – or for how long – who knows? Maybe only until the next transport.

Janek was working as a clerk outside the ghetto and when he returned from work that evening he came to us and asked where his wife and son were. We could hardly bear to face him. He had a terrible shock when we told him. He started screaming, taking out his distress on us for allowing them to go, though of course it was not our fault.

The next day I could scarcely bring myself to look at another child. Janek's son was such a handsome, clever boy, with long, golden hair and the most gorgeous blue eyes. I like to think that because he looked more Aryan than Jewish they may have shown some pity and spared his life.

The day before they went on the transport, my sister-in-law had gone out shopping and bought him a big bag of chocolates and sweets on the black market. It was as if she had a premonition that something bad would happen to them. He said to her: 'Mummy, why are you buying me all these sweets? Don't worry: when the Germans want to shoot me, I will just lie down on the ground and pretend that I am dead.' It shows that even a child of that age – three years old – knew what was going on.

We were aware of the transports leaving for different concen-tration camps and we had heard about people being shot on the way. We did not know how bad conditions were in the camps, because no one ever came back to tell us. Auschwitz was a less familiar name to us then than Mauthausen and Dachau, and we knew that Belsen was a *Vernichtungslager* (extermination camp). But no matter how much information comes your way, until you see for yourself, it is impossible to believe that such things can occur.

My brother was so upset at losing his wife and son that he decided to go to France and join the Partisans of the French Resistance Movement. He wanted me to go as well. He knew somebody who could get us Christian papers. It was a great risk. We would be required to learn all the Christian prayers and study the Bible, in case (as was more than likely) we were rigorously tested on these.

None of our family looked typically Jewish. Had we done so, obtaining such papers would have been out of the question as our appearance would immediately have betrayed our intentions, even before the Germans' religious inquisition got under way.

Janek tried to persuade me to escape with him, but I felt my place was with Mother and my sisters. Miriam was with her 'husband', Hela had no wish to go anywhere else, and Mother's health was not sufficiently robust to cope with the upheaval. In any case, it was not so easy for one person to obtain several sets of papers.

Nonetheless, Janek obtained false papers for the two of us as a standby, and I hid mine underneath the lino in our room, stamped and containing a photograph of me with my hair in plaits.

My brother Willek and his girlfriend Nusia shared a room together in a nearby street. Like our sister Miriam and her 'husband', they had been deeply in love and keen to marry, and Mother arranged another unofficial 'wedding' ceremony, when the rabbi came and gave the couple his blessing.

Willek's friend, Jusef Hollander, a student chemist, had been through a similar ceremony, but shortly afterwards he was sent away on a transport. His 'wife' came over to Willek one morning and said: 'Please do me a favour. Come and help me move this wardrobe.' So he went to her room and stood on a table to lift something down from the top of the wardrobe before moving it. The guards in the street outside saw him, and one of them pointed a gun through the window and shot him.

The news spread within minutes. People ran to tell us that he had been shot and wounded and was on the way to hospital with Nusia in an ambulance. He died before he got there.

Hela and I followed, running behind the ambulance, but they refused to let us into the hospital. We waited outside, and in the afternoon they carried him out on a little trolley. He was draped in a black sheet, which wasn't long enough to cover him completely. I will always remember seeing his legs sticking out from under that sheet. I said: 'No, it can't be. Maybe he is only sleeping.' I was hysterical and wanted to revive him, but they took him away to the cemetery to be buried. He couldn't have a proper funeral, and no one, not even my mother, was allowed anywhere near the cemetery. As always, the Nazis wanted to cover their tracks and everything had to be hush-hush.

For days afterwards I kept going to the window of our room and looking out, thinking: 'Maybe he will come back. Maybe they haven't really killed him.' He was such a gifted fellow, so intelligent. He was my favourite brother and I loved him dearly. I couldn't believe he was dead.

By this time, a terrible fear filled every corner of the ghetto. We felt lost and began to wonder what was the purpose of living. But we had to be prepared for the next episode and to continue our fight for survival.

Every few weeks there were segregations. The Gestapo would come knocking on doors: 'Does so-and-so live here? Come with me.' When they needed more slaves to send to concentration camps in Poland and Germany, they went round gathering up people at random.

As some transports were leaving, others were arriving – from Czechoslovakia, Hungary, Holland.

The older ones among us became increasingly depressed, as they knew they had little hope of surviving. People over 50, unless they looked much younger, didn't have much future.

In the factory I got to know some older married women whose husbands were in England on business, or who had sent their children to study there. I thought: 'What shall I do to cheer them up?' I became a fortune teller, reading people's palms. I had never studied palmistry, but I just used my instinct, a little bit of psychic ability. We used to get together at lunchtime, when it was quiet and there were no German patrols about.

I remember in particular one middle-aged woman whose husband had gone to England. She was missing him and crying every day, so I said to her: 'Come on, let me tell your fortune.' The next thing I knew was that I was surrounded by people, all holding out their hands and saying: 'Tell me! Tell me!'

I became very popular! – and whatever I told them about themselves and their lives turned out to be true. I told them about their character, their backgrounds, having known nothing about them before. They would say to me: 'How did you know that?'

Above all, I told them not to lose hope. I might say: 'Oh yes, it is very hard and you are suffering a great deal, but eventually things will get better' – and so on.

If I saw a tragic future ahead for them, I would never reveal this. I tried not to depress people. I used to say: 'Your husband has been through a lot,' or 'He may be wounded, but he is thinking of you,' and just to see a woman's face light up . . . I felt it was like a special gift given to me.

I wish I had carried on doing it. Now, when I meet anyone new, I try to make my own assessment of that person. My very first impression is always the lasting one. I sum up the person in my mind and I am nearly always proved right.

I am a very good judge of people. Even now, when I go on business trips with Norman, my husband, I stick to first impressions when dealing with clients. I might have doubts about somebody we meet. Norman will say: 'Oh, no, he's not like that.' I say: '*You'll* see . . .' and after a time he realises I am right.

I can see through people. I can tell straight away if they are superficial or putting on an act.

All the time in the ghetto we were hoping that the war would end soon. We read the paper and studied the maps and wondered: 'Where are the Allies? Maybe they will break through *here* – or *here?*'

The newspaper, of course, was heavily censored and a lot of what was printed was speculation, not the truth. There was no news of events in the rest of the world.

Everybody was trying to do their bit, selling or exchanging goods. Hunger changes people to such an extent that they will do anything in order to get food, especially when they have a wife and child to look after, or a mother. And so a loaf of bread, some butter or potatoes played a very important part in our daily lives.

I used to buy cooking oil in quantity from a chemist's shop outside the ghetto, run by friends of my mother. I acted as a kind of courier, carrying the oil back in two-gallon cans to a shop in the ghetto. I earned some commission on this.

It was a very thick, unpurified paraffin oil – consumable but unappetising – and I used to add a bit of colour to it by combining it with another more palatable oil. It was this oil that the female shop owner sold in the ghetto. It was a wonderful source of nourishment for many of us, as we were lacking in fat.

On each of these journeys to and from the ghetto, I showed my pass. I was lucky. I never got stopped and questioned. Many people went out of the ghetto and never returned. They were taken to Nazi HQ, interrogated, beaten up, often hung by the toes, and that was the end of them. Anything could have happened outside the ghetto and no one would have known what had become of me.

We remained in the ghetto for several months, and then we heard that we were being sent to a concentration camp. These camps had originally been referred to as work (or labour) camps, because their function had been to provide various types of factory work to service the German war machine. At first, because of the hardships of the ghetto, we had been led to believe they might offer us a better life. But, as we now suspected and were soon to discover for ourselves, these camps were nothing but giant torture chambers.

Some people escaped from the ghetto through the sewers, but a very small percentage got out alive. By the time my brother Janek went down there, the Gestapo had found out that people were using it as an escape route and, on the other side, where the sewers join the sea, they were waiting with their machine-guns. Several months passed before we had any evidence of what had happened to him.

My papers were still concealed under the lino in our room in the ghetto. A friend of Henek, Miriam's 'husband', was in charge of one of the groups which had been assigned to clear up the houses in the ghetto before it was liquidated. I gave the man a description of these papers, told him exactly where they were and said: 'Get them and burn them.'

Afterwards, I doubted whether this had been a wise move, as it was a risk to trust anybody apart from one's immediate family. However, when we met again at Plaszov camp he assured me that the papers had been destroyed, and this set my mind at rest.

4

See Nothing, Hear Nothing, Feel Nothing

There were posters up all over the ghetto telling us to assemble on 1 March 1942 ready for our departure to Plaszov camp, a distance of about ten kilometres, as the ghetto was about to be liquidated. We packed a few things, just the bare essentials: some warm clothes, underwear, a blanket, toothbrush, brush and comb. Each of us was limited to thirty kilos of belongings, and we were forbidden to have pencils, pens, paper or books in our possession. That was against Nazi 'law'. Anyone caught with a radio was liable to be shot, and I'd heard a story about someone at Mauthausen camp who was hanged for the simple act of reading a newspaper.

All means of identification had been taken away from us: birth certificate, passport, all personal documents.

We lined up in rows of ten, under strict orders not to try to escape, and we walked through the city and beyond, for about three hours.

Plaszov camp was built on the site of a Jewish cemetery. On the left, as we entered the main gate, there was a large office building, heavily guarded. Next to it was a ramp and an outpost where police were stationed. A right turning past that building brought us to a steep hill, and quite a long way up the hill was the Commandant's villa and, nearby, a group of other smart houses where senior Nazi officials lived.

Higher still, on the right, were some big fields, and here rows and rows of barracks were situated, a whole estate of newly-built barracks. Rising up in the distance was a mountain.

Behind the barracks and further up the hill was the latrine block. Beyond that was a long slope and at the far end of this the guards were stationed in their watchtowers.

Each barrack was known as a block and given a number. Mine was block ten. Each block held about a hundred people and was presided over by a *blockowa* (block assistant). There were two tiers of bunks arranged against the walls and window, with another set of bunks in the middle. I slept on the bottom bunk next to the window, with my mother and sisters on either side.

Men and women worked together but lived apart, even if they were married. My sister Miriam worked with her 'husband' during the day but at night they slept in separate barracks.

Most of the time we were at work. Each morning we had to gather at five o'clock in a field which had been set aside as a central square or assembly area. Hundreds of us, men and women in separate groups, used to gather there, sometimes for hours, until Amon Goeth, the camp commandant, deigned to turn up. Then we were counted and allocated jobs for the day.

He might come at seven, eight or nine o'clock – or much later, depending on his mood. He often arrived very drunk and dazed, having come straight from one of the SS officers' all-night parties. While we waited for him, we were expected to stand all the time and in all weathers. The *kapos* guarding us made sure that nobody sat down. Some people fainted from the extreme cold – or heat. Others passed away.

The sight of Goeth approaching always made us tremble. We could see him in the distance striding up to the top of the hill accompanied by two huge, vicious-looking Alsatian dogs and, sometimes, a third dog: white with black spots.

He was a tall, top-heavy man, broad and fat. He sometimes wore a little green hunting cap, pointed at the front, and very high boots, and he carried a long whip. We knew that on days when he was wearing this outfit there would be many casualties among the inmates.

First of all, he would walk over to the men's side. It was so quiet that you could have heard a fly buzzing. The atmosphere was tense and full of fear. We could hear the echo from Goeth's shouting and the growling of the dogs. We could see the way he kept whipping the side of his boots while his bodyguard, who often came with him, fingered his revolver.

Goeth walked slowly by, staring at each man in turn. Often, maybe every few days, he would single some out. He would say: '*You* haven't shaved today' – and shoot the man down. He'd tell another: 'You look too stupid' – and shoot him down. And another: 'You look too clever' – shoot him down. You could hear him counting the numbers of people he had killed.

On a morning like that he might shoot a hundred people, simply to exercise his authority.

He had to walk past where the women were standing, on his way back down the hill, and we were always trembling, terrified that he might try the same tactics on *us*. Fortunately, he didn't.

We went to work. In the early months at Plaszov my mother and I continued to go out to the uniforms factory in the city, along with hundreds of our fellow inmates. Morning and evening, we were escorted by black-uniformed Ukrainian guards and Alsatian dogs. We did alternate weeks of day and night shifts.

Other people used to go out to different kinds of work, using their own specialised skills – carpenters, tailors, pharmacists, architects.

We were all counted on the way to and from work. Some people tried to escape, but they were soon recaptured and brought back to the camp to be given very hard – and, in many cases, fatal – punishment.

It was impossible to escape because all our clothes, even our underclothes, were painted in heavy yellow stripes and we had numbers on our backs. My number was 257 and a fourth digit which I do not recall.

In the beginning, I managed to hide my long plaits under a white scarf, which all women inmates were required to wear, but many people had their heads shaved completely. I remember transports of Jewish women from Hungary and Holland arriving. You could hear the sound of the Dutch women's clogs as they marched into the camp in their striped garments, hideously bald.

There were Polish political prisoners, too. They were based in a different part of the camp, segregated from the Jewish inmates, and they had the letter 'P' on their clothes in front and at the back. I used to see them go to work in the fields, but we were not allowed to speak to one another.

Day and night, transports were coming in from other towns, and day and night the machine guns were in operation. From my bunk I often used to hear the guns firing in the middle of the night. People outside were digging their own graves and being shot into them.

In the night, when you walked from the working quarters to the living quarters, you could smell the bodies burning. They had this specific, terrible smell. There was no crematorium at Plaszov, and so the Nazis made us carry the wood for the bodies to be burned. They burned them straightaway after shooting them. Burned away the evidence.

All the time we were being watched. Goeth's beautiful white villa with picture windows had been built for him by the inmates, and he had the habit of standing at one of the windows with his binoculars. He used to scan the entire camp as far as the outer fields, and if he noticed anyone slacking he would come down, drive to the area and shoot the person. He had his eye on everybody.

Sometimes when I was walking outside, I would happen to look up and see him standing there at the window, so I just carried on walking – very fast, eyes down. One felt continually tense and edgy, wondering: 'Am I doing the right thing?'

Women were expected to do the same heavy labouring jobs as the men. One day my sister Hela was in a group of women sitting breaking tombstones into tiny pieces for building roads. It was in the summer and very hot. Another, older woman was working with Hela. Both of them had hammers and they were breaking the stones in the heat of the day. Goeth appeared. He was watching them closely. He walked past my sister and said to the other woman: 'You are not doing it properly. Get up and I'll show you how.'

So he sat down and started hammering away. Then he got up and said: 'Now *you* do it,' and as she sat down again and began to break the stones, he shot her in cold blood.

To witness the murder of this woman who had been sitting next to her only a moment before was a terrible shock for Hela, but she dared not show her feelings at the time.

Two hours later she returned to the camp, speechless and looking as white as a sheet. It was some time before she felt able to tell us what had happened. We had known the woman well. She had lived in our barrack, on the same side as us.

There were stone mines where inmates, mainly men, were sent as a punishment and never came out alive. They were tortured in there, whipped to death as they were striking the stones. Now and then we could hear the echo coming out of the quarries from the crying and moaning of the men, and we shivered at the thought of what they must have been suffering.

They were sent there for no reason except to gratify the Nazis' sadistic whims. If a person in charge of a group going out to work had counted the numbers incorrectly he would be taken into the mine to be punished.

Through the tiny barred window of my barrack I could see people passing by outside. The searchlights shone through so brightly at night that sleep was difficult. I used to lie on my bunk peering through the window and seeing half-naked men working with tombstones. I could see those poor men stripped to the waist, their bodies soaked in perspiration, walking round and round in a circle carrying those heavy marble stones. The Nazis were whipping them to make them walk faster. The men kept falling and screaming and, because they were screaming, the Nazis went on hitting them.

This went on every night for several months, and all the time the rest of us had to remain silent. The hardest thing was to keep our sanity. We had to pretend that we saw nothing, heard nothing, felt nothing. Even the act of looking out of the window could have resulted in the death penalty.

They had many different ways of torturing the women, too. Once, we had to kneel on the ground and put our heads right down, with our hands over our eyes. We had to stay in that crouched position for about an hour, and during that time all we could hear was the sound of boots marching, the footsteps of men being taken away. How many mothers lost their sons that day? How many wives lost husbands?

The Nazis stopped us from looking because they wanted to avoid any outbursts of violence or hysteria. They were afraid that we might have run screaming and shouting for the men to come back. When we finally did look up, we saw most of them in the distance, marching away from the camp.

On another occasion, we had to strip naked and lean over a long table, baring our bottoms. Goeth walked in and ordered the Ukrainian guards to whip us. These men, strutting around with whips and rifles, were menacing and cruel, with real hate in their eyes.

They gave us fifteen, twenty-five, thirty lashes. The pain was dreadful and, in my own case, the bruises and abrasions were still there after six weeks. If anyone screamed too loudly they were hung up by the ankles, and the Polish doctor, Dr Gross, stood by to mop up the blood.

Although he held quite a senior position in the medical hierarchy at the camp (helping to supervise segregations and working in the hospital), Dr Gross was just a pawn in the Nazis' scheme of things and had to obey orders. When the Ukrainians lashed us, he was not in a position to intervene with the Commandant on our behalf. He may have felt sorry for us, but he was powerless to act without putting his own life at risk.

Every few days a different event would be staged. There was one occasion when they announced they would take all the elderly people and segregate them before sending them on a transport. My mother decided to hide. She went into our barrack, climbed up into her bunk and slipped between the blankets. The covers had to be very straight and smooth. The Nazis expected military standards of discipline and tidiness from the inmates – as if we were in the Army.

When I was quite sure that her bed was sufficiently neat and free of creases to meet those requirements, I left her and went outside.

Mother stayed like that for nearly an hour. Luckily, she was quite slim and nobody noticed she was there. The *blockowa* reported that our barrack was empty, but the Nazis never took the *blockowa*'s word. They always wanted to check everything for themselves, and they went running in like lunatics, shouting, and hitting and punching the blankets and bunks with their rifles and bayonets, looking underneath the bunks and examining every available corner.

After they had finished their search and gone away, my mother stepped down from her bunk. The *blockowa* was amazed to see her and said: 'Where have you been?' She couldn't understand how my mother had managed to remain undetected. We were afraid that she might report the incident to the *kapos* and that word would eventually reach the Commandant but, fortunately for us, she didn't do this.

The *blockowa* was responsible for distributing the ration of bread and for the daily running of the block. She sat at a table under the window. We had to come to the front of the block to receive our ration, and after counting us she reported back to the *kapos* who, in turn, reported to a higher authority.

Although most *blockowas* were Jewish, they kept their distance and never associated with us. It was important to keep in their good books, as they had a certain status in the camp hierarchy. I'm not sure how the system worked but I believe they had to know some of the Jewish *kapos* and to be recommended by them. *Blockowas* had to report to *kapos*, *kapos* were subject to the authority of the head *kapo*. He reported to the Nazis, who informed the Commandant.

The Jewish *kapos* wore uniforms. I could not understand their mentality. The readiness of some of them to collaborate with the Nazis to save their own skins shows how much influence the Germans had, and how easy it was for them to be corrupted and to lose their sense of morality.

After a few months, the camp began to resemble a miniature town: self-sufficient, well-equipped and highly organised. It was like a conveyor belt. They laid on a railway line which ran right into the camp alongside the main gate and enabled people to be loaded straight on to the trucks, thus affording easy access in and out of the camp. A whole complex of barracks had been established as working quarters: carpentry and meat stores, uniform factories (separate barracks for officers' and soldiers' uniforms). Few people now went outside the camp to work. Most of the work carried out in the camp had some connection with the war and the Germans' defence requirements, and we were the slaves, hired – for no wages – to further their cause.

Meanwhile, more segregations took place, particularly of older inmates. How my mother continued to survive was a miracle. I remember another occasion, when she was working at her machine in the camp factory and suddenly she felt a hand hit her on the back of her neck. She turned round and there was Jon, Goeth's assistant, a little fellow who could be even more objectionable than Goeth.

Mother asked him: 'Why are you hitting me?' People working there were astonished at her reaction. So, too, was Jon himself.

'What is your name?' he said.

'Estera Goldfinger,' she shouted back at him.

'Huh!' he said, and walked away.

Everyone was speechless. Mother thought he would put her on a list for the next transport, but thank goodness it came to nothing. He could have taken her away there and then and shot her.

She had such a powerful personality, such an impact on people, that maybe, in some strange way, the Nazis respected that. They sought obedience from the inmates but perhaps they liked the fact that Mother was so proud, so spontaneous, so sure of herself.

Jon used to prowl around the camp, inspecting the workshops, kitchens and food stores, checking up on the workers. He deputised for Goeth in his absence, coming to the square for the morning assembly and mass count.

The Nazis were meticulous about accuracy and numbers, sometimes waking us up at two in the morning to be counted. Many of the worst atrocities took place during the night, when we were most exhausted from the hard work of the day.

I do not think that anyone, whatever the situation, could ever experience the same degree of continuous fear that we lived through under Nazi rule. The fear of what might have happened to us the previous day and what might be in store for us tomorrow. We would go to bed hoping to be able to rest, but in our dreams we relived the things that had happened during that day. We would go to bed with fear and wake up in the morning with it, because each day marked a new, different and often more deadly set of horrors.

I was one of the youngest inmates there, but I was tall and looked older than my years – and that was to my advantage. A child had to act much older in order to survive. After a time, children under fifteen were automatically sent straight to the gas chambers and killed.

I became much older in my ways, in my disposition. I aged quickly because of the burden of worry and sorrow that I carried around the whole time and the uncertainty of what the next minute might bring. All this preyed on our minds and nerves.

The insecurity of our daily existence made people so serious both in their general outlook and in their physical appearance. There was no smile, no brightness in their eyes, no fun.

We were not allowed to cry or show our feelings. The agony grew deep inside me and I became like a stone.

I saw a 14-year-old Polish boy hanged, just because he was singing. A guard who was passing the boy's barrack heard him singing 'God Save the King', dragged him out and beat him up.

The following day extra police were summoned, guards with their dogs were stationed at regular points around the camp, and machine guns were positioned on the ground around the edge of the camp as well as on top of the watchtowers. They built a scaffold in the main square. Thousands of us gathered there. We saw the boy being taken to be hanged. He was crying out: 'Please let me live. I am only 14 years old. I have done nothing. My mother and sister have been shot. Leave me alone. I will never sing another song again.'

The guards pushed him forward with their rifles, and we were all made to face the rope, which was placed around his neck. They pulled him up three times, and let him down again. Eventually, when he was half-dead, one of the guards drew a pistol and shot him in the back of the neck.

Later that day, three men were hanged in the same spot, one by one. We were made to watch this, too. One of the men was so heavy that the rope broke and they had to get another one.

The following day, as we walked to the factory, we passed an open lorry coming up the hill, full of priests, and behind them another lorry full of nuns. Half an hour later, we heard the distant sound of machine guns, followed by loud screams, and we said to ourselves: 'Another sacrifice has been made.' It shocked us a great deal, as we realised to what extent the Nazis' net of victims was widening.

Like numerous others, they had had to undress and dig their own graves. And, like the rest, their clothes were brought to the factory afterwards, to be cleaned up and mended.

Transports kept coming in, and Goeth used to collect jewellery and other valuables from the new inmates. Many cases full of watches, rings and other treasure were discovered later in his villa, items that he was supposed to have delivered to the German government but that he selected for himself. Shortly before we left Plaszov we heard that he had been found out and arrested. After the war he was taken into the main square in Cracow and hanged.

If he hadn't been caught, I am sure that he would have fled the country and lived a life of idle luxury in exile, changing his name and perhaps his appearance, too, as so many senior SS officials have done since the war.

The Nazis made us hand over our few remaining possessions of any value. They warned us that anyone who failed to do so would be shot. They wanted silver, gold, any precious metal. We had sewn things into our clothes which we did not want to part with, a trick which the Nazis soon discovered.

A group of guards came into the barrack and turned our bunks upside down, pulling off the blankets and scattering the straw mattresses. They rushed in with their knives and scissors and tore everything up. They even ripped the shoulder pads off the women's dresses. This went on for a whole day, during which time we were forbidden to leave the barrack, not even to go to the toilet.

My sister, Miriam, had fastened her 'wedding' ring and watch into the shoulder pads of her dress. My mother, too, had a watch sewn into one of her shoulder pads, and some dollar notes tucked inside a man's tie (dollars were worth more than zlotis).

The guards kept emphasising that this was our last chance to hand over our possessions. We had to come forward and throw everything into a large container, like a trunk, at one end of the barrack.

The Ukrainians came in and carried the trunks from each block to the main stores, where they were kept under special guard.

That evening an elderly woman, who slept in a bunk on the opposite side of my barrack, committed suicide by taking poison. She was the mother of Dr Gross, the Polish doctor. We wondered how the Nazis would react to this woman's suicide, and whether they would decide to shoot us all.

Some people were so shocked and upset at this latest indignity – the loss of their precious belongings– that they tried to escape, but they didn't get far. Most of them electrocuted themselves on the wire fencing. Others were shot by the guards in their watchtowers. Throughout the night we heard the familiar, awful sound of machine guns.

No one, to my knowledge, ever succeeded in escaping completely. Many tried, while they were working outside the camp, but they were soon found, dragged back and tortured – often in front of a mass audience of inmates.

I remember this happening to one particular girl. The guards brought her back and marched her into the square where we were all assembled. There was an SS woman whom we nicknamed *Hlopka* (meaning 'riff-raff'). She was tall, mannish and extremely strong. She grabbed this girl by the hair and threw her around the square, beating and kicking her as if she was cleaning a blanket. She made the girl stand up on a chair, then pushed her down on to the ground. We were forced to watch this chilling scene over and over again, while the guards just stood by and laughed.

It would have been better if they had shot her right away and saved her suffering but, as always, the guards delighted in torturing people.

Meanwhile, at the command of the guards, another woman inmate was playing the violin and singing a sentimental song in German ('Come Back My Sweetheart').

On the evening after the raid on our barracks, as I lay on my bunk next to the window I could see, in the dazzle of the searchlights, a half-naked man being hit repeatedly by the guards. The man kept falling over and every time he attempted to get up they struck him again.

We were left with little except the clothes we were wearing. We had become beggars, but we comforted ourselves with the thought that if we were ever free again, we would be able to get by. We had learned to be resourceful.

The following day, as usual, we went to work in the factory. By this time a complex of uniforms factories had been set up within the camp itself and none of us working there was allowed beyond the camp boundaries. This meant an end to bartering. Gone was the opportunity of exchanging something for a sausage or a loaf of bread which could be smuggled back to the camp at the end of a shift.

It also meant an end to my 'clairvoyance' sessions in the lunch-hours, as we were more closely supervised working inside the camp than we had been outside it. Life became very, very grim.

The Jewish foreman was still in charge, but the Nazis would come with their dogs to check up on us, especially on the night shift. They would stand and listen outside the barrack and look through the windows to make sure everybody was working.

One night, in the next work barrack, they noticed a woman worker talking to somebody. A guard went in, hauled her out and the dogs tore her to pieces. We could hear the barking and the shrieking, and after we left work we saw trails of blood on the ground outside. When we heard and saw such things, we wondered who was going to be next.

My sister Miriam still worked outside the camp, with her 'husband', an architect who was in charge of a group of skilled Jewish workers. Miriam was his secretary, the only woman in a team of fifty-five men, mainly professional people such as solicitors and medical students. They were working on a building in the main square in Cracow.

Miriam had cooking facilities there, and she used to bring food back to the camp for us. Every time we met she used to say to me: 'I will try to get you a job so that you can come out to work with us.' She felt sorry for me being shut away in the camp, and told me that in a couple of days I would be able to join them. She said that on the following day (14 September) at 7.30 p.m., she would come and see me again and give me the details. 'My heart aches that you are there.' These were her last words to me.

I was working on the night shift. It was getting dark and I was standing at the window waiting for Miriam before starting work. Suddenly I heard the sound of machine guns from the direction of the mountain. A strange feeling came over me. I turned away from the window for a few moments, then walked back there again, listening. I heard more shots, and then it went quiet.

I waited and waited, and still she didn't come. About half an hour later people were arriving for the night shift. Groups were forming. They were talking together and looking at me. I asked what had happened. They answered: 'Nothing. Nothing.' Each time I approached a group of people they gradually stopped talking. My anxiety was growing, and I sensed that something was wrong and that it had some connection with me.

Finally, a woman revealed that a group of workers had been shot. A Jewish *kapo* told me that it was the group with whom Miriam had been working, and that both she and her 'husband' had been shot.

Apparently, Miriam and the men had been caught bringing food into the camp. They were searched at the gate, and when the food was discovered Goeth gave the order for them to be shot. They were marched off to the mountain, and had to strip naked and dig their own graves. Miriam had asked if she could say goodbye to her 'husband', and when they were in each other's arms they were shot together into the grave.

I cried so much that night that I would have filled endless buckets with my tears. I was lying on the floor in a corner, sobbing among a pile of uniforms. My fellow workers were so affected by this latest tragedy that they rallied round and tried to help, and one of them took over my machine to cover for me on the night shift.

In the morning I wondered how I could break the news to my mother, who was on a different shift, but she already knew. Somebody else had told her.

We tried to comfort each other as best we could, and we longed for some privacy so that we could feel free to express our grief more openly.

Miriam used to sleep on my left side in the barrack and, from that moment to this, my left arm has always felt chilly, as if a part of my flesh had been cut away from me.

5

'I Only Have One Mother'

It was the tradition for relatives to participate in the Nazis' ritual of death, and the day after my sister and her 'husband' were shot, we had to carry the wood for the bodies to be burned, my mother and sister Hela and I together. As always, the Nazis wanted to destroy every trace of evidence from their crimes.

Our period of mourning was not long, because there was always some new diversion being dreamed up by our captors for their amusement and our humiliation.

That same afternoon, a group of *kapos* led by Hilovitch, their chief, came into the barracks looking for older people. They called out my mother's name, 'Estera Goldfinger', and ordered her to accompany them to the segregations shed. As they were taking her away, I leaned out of the window of the barrack and begged them to leave her alone.

'Haven't you got enough out of me? Yesterday, my sister and her husband were shot. Today you want to take my mother. Have some mercy.' The *kapos* said nothing and turned away. It was like talking to a brick wall.

Then I saw Dr Gross walking down the hill towards the shed, and I pleaded with him to save her. A word from him might influence the Nazis' final decision. He might say to the guard standing next to him: 'She is healthy and can work.'

I gave him my mother's name. He said he would see what he could do but doubted whether he could achieve much.

I was filled with despair and uncertainty. I wandered restlessly around the side of the barrack to the latrines block behind, and back again. Resigned, I sat on my bunk thinking, 'She will never come back.'

About an hour later I heard shouting from outside. Some girls came running into the barrack and said: 'Your mother's coming back.' I rushed out of the door and couldn't believe my eyes when I saw her running back up the hill to the barrack. She looked and felt like a reborn person.

She told us later that she had been herded together with dozens of other women and men, all middle-aged or elderly, in the big shed. Each one handed over a keepsake to the *kapos*. One took out a watch and said: 'Would you give this to my daughter?' Another: 'Give these few zlotis [pence] to my son.' They were weeping because they knew they were going to be shot. The Nazis were stationed outside the shed with their rifles, waiting to march them off to the mountain to their deaths.

All the time Mother kept pushing her way towards the door. She managed to reach Dr Gross and said: 'My name is Mrs Goldfinger. Let me out of here.' He said: 'Go on up to your barrack,' and back she came. A few others returned with her, but those who stayed behind were taken away and we heard shots ringing out after she returned to the barrack.

It was a chance in a million that she got away, and I was overjoyed to see her again, but also very upset that so many others had perished. When it came to segregations, the Nazis wasted no time. They took every opportunity to organise a party of people to be shot.

On another occasion, all the women in the camp had to strip naked and assemble in the main square. It was April and still very cold. There was a row of long tables and, sitting at them, a panel of high-ranking Nazi women and men.

We had to line up and walk forward, one by one, and jump over a series of large holes in the ground, holes that had been specially dug to test our level of physical fitness – and therefore our 'right' to survival.

It was like some sort of contest, a cattle market. We were frightened to look at the 'judges'. We just looked down at our feet as we marched past in a straight line. Those who stumbled or fell into the holes were automatically segregated.

They could see from our bodies approximately what ages we were. They made notes and took names. My mother, because she was older and had poor eyesight, tripped, and her name was added to the list of people relegated to the next transport.

This transport, I learned later, was going to the gas chambers at Auschwitz. A friend of mine, who worked in the office where the lists were compiled, told me in confidence that my mother's name was definitely on that list.

A few weeks later word came that a transport was due to depart, and those who had been named had to assemble one morning in the square. We all met there at 5 a.m. as usual, and waited until Commandant Goeth arrived and the mass count and roll-call took place. My name was called and I went off to work, but my mother's name had still not been called. I was walking down the hill to the factory with some friends when I saw the head of the medical department, a big fellow who looked as if he could have been Goeth's brother.

I said to the other girls: 'I am going to ask him if he will leave my mother alone.' One of them said: 'How could you dare to do that?' But I didn't care. I had nothing to lose, because my mother meant so much to me. Without her, there would have been nothing left for me to live for. I felt that even if he shot me, at least I had tried my best to save her.

So I walked over to the man and spoke to him in my best German. I said: 'Look – I only have one mother. Please save her. She is still a young woman and she works very hard.' He looked surprised at my audacity, and said the final decision was not up to him but the camp commandant. He told me to go back to work.

At work I found it impossible to concentrate, as my mind was so full of the suffering my mother might have to face. All day I had no news of her.

ABOVE LEFT: My brother Janek, who was never seen again after trying to escape through the sewers of the ghetto in 1940. Later his green fisherman's waistcoat was discovered among a pile of clothes in one of the central stores in Plaszov concentration camp.

ABOVE: My sister Miriam, aged 17, outside our house in Cracow. Later she and her husband were caught trying to bring food into Plaszov camp and shot in 1941. She used to sleep on my left side in the barrack, and from that moment to this my left arm has always felt chilly.

LEFT: Willek, the youngest of my brothers, was shot in the ghetto in May 1940 while helping to move furniture for his sister-in-law.

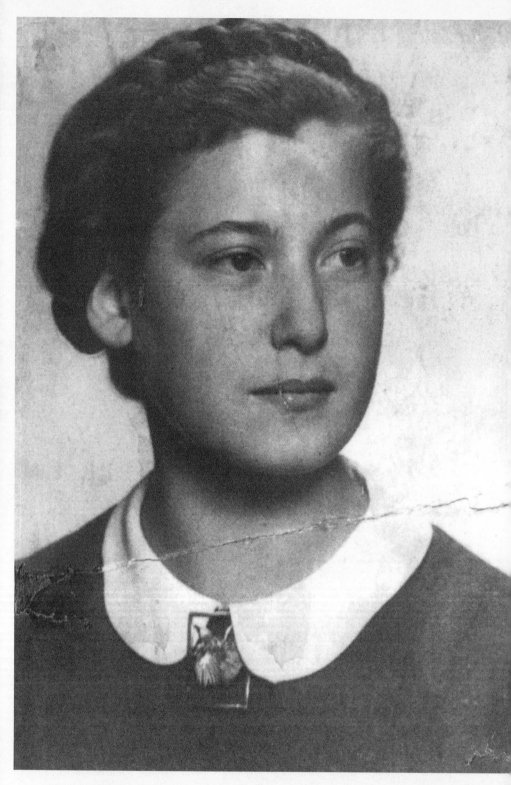

This photograph was taken of me in spring 1939, when I was 16 years old and still had my long plaits.

My mother after her typhus illness, in June 1945. She is standing outside a barrack near Bergen, after being moved from Belsen concentration camp.

INSET: My mother at home in England on her birthday, 8 December 1948.

ABOVE: The liberation of Belsen, April 1945. British troops had to keep the SS guards apart from the women internees. This photograph was taken a week after the Army entered the camp. © *Imperial War Museum/Robert Hunt Library*

BELOW: The British Army set light to the typhus-infected, lice-ridden huts at Belsen. The last hut is seen here burning to the ground on 21 May 1945. © *Imperial War Museum/Robert Hunt Library*

I finished work at about seven in the evening. A woman I knew from my barrack came to see me to give me the news that my mother was alive and had not been sent away. She was working on the night shift, and the following morning, about 5 o'clock, I went to see her. I thanked God she was safe, but I also wondered for how much longer. Until the next transport?

At least she was working. Working kept you alive. As long as they could make use of you in some way, you were probably safe.

Being able to speak fluent German was a great advantage at Plaszov. When I pleaded with that Nazi doctor for my mother's freedom, he was astonished that I spoke such good German, and perhaps that made an impact. Had I simply stood there gesticulating at him, I would have made very little impression.

I was longing to listen to a radio or read a newspaper, but such things were only dreams to all of us. We desperately wanted to know what was happening in the world, but here in the camp we were helpless people, at the mercy of those with the guns and the power. We often wondered what ordinary people were doing abroad while we remained shut away.

Sometimes, while walking around the camp, we heard snatches of German broadcasts from the Nazis' radios. We could hear Hitler's voice booming out, boasting of how the world would fall at his feet and how he aimed to speak from Buckingham Palace. Eventually, we were so brainwashed that we even thought: 'Maybe he will achieve that.' We heard rumours that Germany was bombing London and we were terrified.

We tried to listen for news of how the war was progressing and we wondered: 'What is the Red Cross doing about our plight? What is England – or America – doing about it? Surely there must be *some* people who will take pity on us?'

If other countries had known of the atrocities that went on in the camps and how many thousands of people lost their lives each year, they might have tried to finish the war more quickly instead of hanging on for six years. We began to think it would never end.

The solace of books was also denied us. I am sure that reading would have been a tonic, a way of entering a different world away from the daily struggle for survival.

The only consolation was to remember the life one used to live. We would talk about old times, my mother, sister Hela and I, whenever we had the chance. It was difficult to converse freely as camp life was so controlled, and the mental release of expressing our feelings on paper was also forbidden us.

Later on, it became even more dangerous to talk openly, as the SS began splitting up families. According to Nazi ideology, all Jews must be unattached and the generations destroyed. We had to be very discreet and in time we learned to conceal any blood ties. Some people knew we were mother, sister and daughter, but fortunately nobody betrayed us.

At Plaszov I was acquainted with many of the inmates, and trusted them. Some were women who had lived in or around Cracow, women whom my mother and I had known for several years. There was one particular woman and her daughter from Cracow with whom we used to share our food.

This was a great source of support to me and my sister, especially on those occasions when Mother's life had been in grave danger after a segregation. Some of these old friends would run to tell me that she was safe.

As the months passed, through being in such close daily contact with each other and sleeping in barracks together, one also got to know other, new inmates. There was great harmony among people. Despair brought us together and we all felt for one another.

Yet, at the same time, there was much jealousy and bitterness. Some women would say to me: 'Your mother came back and mine didn't.' One had to tread carefully, as so many of them lost their loved ones. In every transport another mother or father was sent away forever.

Every incident was magnified – exaggerated – in the unnatural circumstances we were in. I was afraid to show my feelings of joy at

my mother's safe return, afraid to say: 'Thank God she survived.'
Mother would whisper to me: 'Sssh! Quiet. Don't say anything.' But I could see the others, recently bereaved, look at
me and I could sense what they were thinking. This was an
extra burden to bear. On the one hand, I was happy that my
mother was alive, but on the other I would be aware of other
people's envy.

After my sister Miriam was shot, I said to them: 'Look – four
of my family have gone already' to try and make them see things
in perspective. I think it helped them to know that, although my
mother had survived, she had lost several children and suffered
much pain.

I tried to find out if my brother Janek really had been shot in
the sewers under the ghetto. I clung to a shred of hope that he
might have escaped after all, and during my lunch-hour at the
factory I often used to go outside to look for him. But Fridka's
brother, who worked in the central store at Plaszov, had recognised
Janek's fisherman's green waistcoat. It was several months before
he had the courage to tell me this. I was heartbroken.

Now, out of our large family, only my mother, my sister Hela,
and I were still together.

Transports continued to come in from other camps, while
others left for a new and often unknown destination, mixing and
separating the people.

We lost track of time. Some days we felt low, but other days
we felt a spark of hope that the Allies would come to our aid. It
was no good being too pessimistic, or we would have destroyed
ourselves.

My one aim was to keep my mother alive, so that I would be
able to tell any other relatives who survived the war: 'There you
are – I saved her.' Maybe this is how I was blessed with the
strength to carry on.

Mother was remarkable and as determined as I was that she
should survive. She got depressed at times but tried not to show
me if she was in tears as she didn't want to depress *me*.

I saw people losing their minds, getting hysterical, suicidal; mothers flinging themselves against the wire because they couldn't bear to be parted from their children. Hundreds of children were taken away overnight from the *Kinderhaus* (nursery). Once, when I was walking in the camp grounds, I looked up and saw one of the SS women loading children very fast into open trucks. They were screaming and crying, and the trucks drove off at great speed, like machine guns firing.

I remember one mother in my barrack who took off her daughter's coat, put it on herself and went to Auschwitz instead of her.

I can remember feeling so desperate, so disillusioned at various times that I even contemplated changing my religion. Why, I wondered, did the Jewish people have to suffer – to be punished? For what?

My mother said prayers every day to bolster me and help me through my crisis of faith. She never lost her faith throughout the war years, not for one moment.

When I saw the things that went on in the camp – the hanging of that young boy, the shooting of priests and nuns, the continual violence against innocent people – I used to pray in my own way to come through it and to be able to talk about it one day. I prayed each evening and my prayer was always the same: 'God, listen to my voice.'

Today, I feel much stronger in my religious beliefs, but I often ask the questions: 'Why did members of my family lose their lives? Why can't people live in harmony? Why can't we all be equal?' There are no answers, and I do not attempt to analyse the matter.

Those of us on night shift at the factory tried to sleep during the day, but this was almost impossible because of the noise and commotion going on around us: machine guns firing, loud voices announcing a forthcoming inspection. Many were the times when we would have to set to and scrub the barrack floor in readiness for inspections by the guards. We lay on our bunks dozing, half-alert, afraid that our names would be called out on some pretext or other.

There was no such thing as rest or peace of mind. On our way back from work to the living quarters, we might be forced to break stones, be kidnapped to the hospital for medical experiments, or hauled off to clean the lavatories.

The latrine block was extremely primitive, consisting of a row of about twenty holes along a single wooden seat. Some people climbed underneath those holes to hide from the Nazis and this saved their lives.

I worked in the uniform factory for over a year. Then, one day, when we were assembled in the barrack to be counted, the *blockowa* asked: 'Who likes dogs?' I put my hand up. I recalled my mother's pet Alsatian at home in Cracow and I was fond of dogs. Some of the other girls and women also volunteered. Several 'dog minders' were needed by top SS officials in the camp.

At first, knowing how vicious the dogs could be, I felt rather dubious about taking on such a job, but once I had shown an interest and been singled out, I could not back down.

I was put in charge of three dogs: Rolf, an Alsatian; Luxi, a big black dog with a fine, silky coat and long tail; and Bingo, a bulldog. They all belonged to Frau Michaels, the mistress of a man called Neuschel who was in charge of the working quarters. He had a child and his wife divided her time between Vienna and Plaszov.

The dogs had a special room all to themselves in the house, a smart villa quite high up the hill.

I had to take them for long walks round the fields, cook their meals, bath them regularly and generally see to their every need. It was very much a full-time occupation. I started work at 5.30 in the morning, and as soon as I arrived I had to clear up their mess. Then I went to collect their ration of best beef from the camp slaughterhouse. I came back and boiled the meat in a big saucepan, with some potatoes and gravy.

Before giving it to the dogs, I fished out some chunks of meat and potatoes and put them aside to give to my mother and some friends. The meat smelled so beautiful and I shall never forget the taste of those potatoes. Just a taste was enough for me. I didn't worry so much for myself. I felt that Mother needed it more than I did. My fulfilment came from the knowledge that she was not starving.

The opportunity of getting extra food was one of the attractions of the job. It was a godsend. The meat had to be of the top quality, as the Nazis treated their animals better than human beings.

About twice a week, when I was out walking the dogs, I used to take a saucepan of food with me, hiding it under my coat. When I saw somebody I knew going towards the working quarters, I called them over and asked: 'Would you please take this to my mother?' If I had a spare minute, I dashed there myself, but usually I was too occupied and couldn't leave the dogs.

My mother shared the food around with Hela and others in our barrack. We couldn't eat on our own because people would look at us and make us feel guilty. We were all in the same boat and so we had to share what little we had.

Some people did gardening, others worked in the fields. Whatever the kind of work, everyone always tried to bring something back to the camp to exchange. Frau Michaels had a little garden where she grew tomatoes and now and then I picked a couple and smuggled them back to our barrack in the evening.

A Polish girl worked near Frau Michaels' house. Her name was Marisia and she was a political prisoner, with the letter 'P' on her clothes, but she never disclosed why she had been sent to Plaszov. She passed me every day, pushing a trolley full of logs, and we used to exchange a few words.

After some weeks I found out that she was working as a housekeeper in one of the SS houses. Several months later we heard that she had been released. She never revealed how she had managed to change jobs. Jewish prisoners were frightened to mix with political prisoners, because we never knew for certain whether they were being used to spy on us or trick us in some way.

Polish political prisoners were treated far better than we were. They were given more frequent changes of clothes and more frequent rations of better quality food: bread, meats, sausage (*Blutwurst* – a kind of black pudding).

There was no one supervising me and no gates to worry about, no searches. Frau Michaels was out for most of the day, working in an office in a different part of the camp. Apart from the occasional glimpse of Commandant Goeth in his villa, I felt much freer.

There were many dogs in the camp. All the high Nazi officials had them and recruited various inmates to look after them. It was considered a privilege to be in charge of dogs but, to us, especially in the freezing Polish winters, it could seem more like punishment.

Sometimes I let the dogs off their leashes and they ran off, and I had to call them back. If anything had happened to them I would have been in serious trouble, so it was a great responsibility. I was constantly worried in case they went too close to the electrically wired fence and I had to watch them the whole time.

When they were on the lead, it was difficult to hold on to them without losing my balance. They were such huge, heavy dogs that they almost pulled me over. They had more strength than I did!

They must have been trained in a rather peculiar way, especially Bingo, the bulldog. Whenever he saw any of the other inmates he used to run towards them, jumping up at them and growling. This scared and upset me a lot. 'Sorry, sorry,' I kept saying. I quickly learned to hold him back on the lead.

The dogs were quite friendly towards me, apart from one occasion when they had a fight in the house. Instead of pouring water over them, I tried to pull them apart and they bit me on the leg. I still have a scar to show for it. My leg was terribly painful, but I had to carry on as if nothing had happened. People never made a fuss about things like that, which were trivial compared with the way the Nazis treated us. The main aim was not to draw too much attention to ourselves. As long as they left us alone, as long as we stayed alive, that was all that mattered.

I had no access to bandages or gauze and had to improvise with a piece of cloth. I tried to keep the wound on my leg clean by washing it regularly with salted water and a little iodine, but it did not heal up properly until after the war was over.

At the end of the day, Frau Michaels would inspect the dogs carefully. She was a tall woman in her mid-thirties, with dark hair and a pale complexion which she plastered with make-up. She barely spoke but was strict and intimidating, very sure of herself.

I had to be polite but keep to myself. It was a case of 'Good morning' and then down to work immediately. Sometimes she would acknowledge me, sometimes she would ignore me. Nevertheless, even though I had no direct appreciation from her, Frau Michaels knew she had to depend on me for the welfare of her dogs and, like many German people, she cared passionately about animals – to the point of sentimentality.

At weekends she often slept until two in the afternoon, or even later. I would have to try and bring the dogs back from their walk much later than usual, otherwise the house would be all locked up and we couldn't get in.

Another of my daily duties was to clean every pair of shoes and boots belonging to Frau Michaels and her partner – and between them there were many.

One winter's evening in 1943, when she was out, I managed to listen to a Polish broadcast from London. A friend of mine who worked in the fields nearby came in and we switched on the radio. There was the familiar 'V for Victory' signal on the airwaves. We heard that transports were leaving for Treblinka camp. We had been hoping for some indication that the war was drawing to a close, and this news gave us very little hope.

We only dared listen for a few minutes, in case somebody noticed and reported us.

I remember one cold winter's morning when I was walking up the hill to Frau Michaels' house. It was like walking on smooth glass, with nothing to grip or hold on to, and I was slipping and sliding, almost on all fours. The ground was hard and glassy like a sheet of ice, and it would have been easy to break a leg.

When I came down again that evening the ice had melted, but with the early morning frost the ground was treacherous.

On another occasion, I had just returned to the house after taking the dogs for their walk. It was a very cold day and I saw four girls picking crops in the fields. I said: 'Come in and warm yourselves.'

They were sitting in the kitchen and I was making them a hot drink when, suddenly, I heard footsteps. I said: 'Quick! Get down in the cellar.'

The trap door leading to the cellar was covered by a piece of carpet. I lifted this up and they climbed down the steps. I had no time to replace the carpet before Frau Michaels came in. She looked at me rather suspiciously and asked: 'Who's here? What's going on?'

'Nothing, nothing,' I said. I must have looked very nervous. In case she referred to the piece of carpet, I told her I'd just been doing some cleaning.

I hoped she wouldn't decide to search the place. But she was in a hurry. She had come to fetch something she had forgotten. She went into her bedroom, and after a few moments came out again with whatever she had been looking for. Then, without another word, she left the house to return to her work.

I can't imagine what I would have done if she had decided to stay there for the rest of the day. Those girls were supposed to go back to their work in the fields, and they would have had to be counted at the end of the day. If they had failed to turn up, we would all have been in trouble.

I had no diary but I was able to keep track of the months by looking at the calendars in Frau Michaels' house. One of the main Jewish festivals is Yom Kippur (the Day of Atonement), which takes place in October. I celebrated this festival in 1944 with Karola Weber, a Jewish friend of mine, who worked nearby as a cleaner/housekeeper for an SS official. We fasted for twenty-four hours. Towards the following evening we waved to one another and Karola came into 'my' house where, in the absence of Frau Michaels, we broke the fast and enjoyed some refreshment together: a cup of coffee and some bread. It was a wonderful feeling, being able to observe that fast.

On another occasion we shared an onion sandwich. We cut up some pieces of onion, placed them between two slices of dry bread and called it Vitamin C.

Karola was a lot older than me – in her twenties – but age mattered less than harmony and understanding between people.

From the age of nine I had had long hair down to my waist. After war broke out I wore it in two plaits across my head, concealing them under a hood or the customary white scarf worn by Jewish women inmates. About a year after we entered Plaszov the Nazis introduced a new ruling that all the women must have their hair cut short and then gather for inspection. I did not obey this order. The sight of those Dutch and Hungarian women with their heads shaved had appalled me so much that I vowed to hang on to my plaits for as long as possible. But one evening, when I was out with the dogs, the wife of Hilovitch, the head *kapo*, noticed that I still had my plaits. She said: 'You must have those plaits cut off. I don't want to see them tomorrow.'

An elderly inmate from the men's block who had been cutting the women's hair came and cut off my plaits. They were lovely thick plaits, and I was really upset about losing them. I left them in Frau Michaels' cellar, thinking that perhaps I might be able to go back and get them sometime. I didn't have the heart to burn them.

Everyone in the camp had to carry out their own job, the profession for which they had been trained. As well as barbers, there were carpenters, tailors, dentists (who had to remove the gold teeth from the corpses) and doctors, like Dr Gross and Dr Schindler, who both worked in the hospital.

Early one summer's morning I was on my way to work at Frau Michaels' house when I saw Goeth at the gate. Soon afterwards, I saw a wagon with a Ukrainian driver, and Hilovitch, the commander of the *kapos*, sitting in the back. I noticed that they had some wooden packing cases on the wagon.

I went on up the hill to fetch the dogs for their morning walk. Later, Karola and I saw a group of guards coming towards the buildings in our part of the camp. They then turned right and grabbed a girl called Gutta who was working nearby. Gutta was Hilovitch's mistress. They marched her down the hill, two guards on either side of her.

By about five o'clock in the afternoon, after we had finished work, we heard that there had been some executions. We had to go to the square and march past a row of bodies lying there on the ground. There was Hilovitch, his short blonde wife, his mistress Gutta, his assistant *kapo*, and another woman.

They had been trying to escape in the wooden boxes we had seen on the wagon. They had got as far as the main gates, where Goeth was waiting. He opened the cases and there they were. He and his guards had lined them up and shot them.

The entire camp – thousands of us – were made to walk several times past the bodies, look closely at them and absorb the full horror of the scene. In front of the bodies was a big poster which said: 'These are the war mongers.'

Goeth told us: 'These people tried to escape. This is a lesson about what will happen to you if any of you try to do the same.'

So that was the end of Hilovitch. Apparently, the Ukrainian guard, who must have given him away to the Nazis, was not shot.

We tried to avoid having any dealings with the *kapos*, or being under any obligation to them, as they were not to be trusted. The only exception to this rule was that time when I pleaded with them to save my mother's life when they were marching her away from the barrack.

One morning, when I returned to the barrack after the night shift, Hela was not there. We learned from the *blockowa* that one of the women guards had kidnapped her and taken her to the main camp hospital, where they experimented on her. They drew the blood out of her body and injected her with petrol. Hela herself told us later that she had been lying on her bunk and beginning to go to sleep when some women guards came in and told her to get dressed and go with them.

At first, Mother and I were forbidden to visit her. I remember speaking to a nurse through the bars of the hospital entrance. She was Jewish, a plumpish girl with glasses. I asked her how Hela was, and she replied: 'I can't tell you a lot, but don't worry – she is all right.'

The nurse was not in a position to reveal what the doctors were doing there, and it was only after several months, when Hela came out of hospital and went back to work in one of the uniforms factories (a separate block from mine), that we realised just how ill she was. She was dragging her feet along and could hardly walk. She had no energy and she was losing a lot of blood.

She was sent to a different, smaller hospital, more like a clinic, and given blood tests. It was only then, through Dr Schindler, the Polish doctor who was treating her, that we discovered that Hela had been a victim of the Nazis' notorious medical experiments.

Who knows what they were trying to prove? I suppose they wanted to use people as guinea pigs, to see how long they could survive.

Now that they had finished with Hela, I was allowed to visit her. Every evening I went to the hospital and tried to keep cheerful and not show her that I knew how sick she was.

Dr Schindler was pleasant and helpful, but he could do little for her as there were not enough medicines to alleviate her symptoms, let alone cure her – and he had less authority than Dr Gross.

Each day she grew weaker. She had been the most beautiful

girl, with features like a model. Now, because of regular injections of petrol, she was unable to move her arms or legs. Her bone marrow and kidneys were deteriorating and she developed TB in her bones.

I heard that she was likely to be sent to Auschwitz, and I tried – through friends – to keep her name off the list.

Then, in December 1944, word came that the camp was about to be liquidated. More and more of the SS were needed at the Front. We heard that Auschwitz was to be our next destination and that we were to leave that very day.

Two nights before we left, I watched a huge transport of men leave the camp. From my bunk in the barrack I could see endless rows of legs marching away. This seemed a bad sign. Many other transports had already been leaving regularly for Buchenwald, Dachau and Mauthausen camps, but not in such large numbers. They used to line up next to the railway line near the main gate, but the numbers of people on this transport were much too great to be accommodated on the trucks.

Our transport, two days later, was equally large and so we, too, had to leave on foot, the last transport from Plaszov.

6

'You've Escaped from the Furnace'

On the morning we were told to leave for Auschwitz, I was at work and there was no time to collect any belongings. Everyone had to assemble in the square, ready for departure.

It was December 1944 and the temperature was about 20 degrees below freezing. I had to go exactly as I was, in the clothes I was standing up in: dress, coat, boots, a thin pair of knickers and stockings. There was no chance at all to grab any warmer layers of clothing, not even extra underwear. I carried a small zipped bag containing the barest essentials.

Those who had time to prepare for the journey put on two, or even three, pairs of stockings, but I had only one pair and the frost bit right through them. That is probably why I suffer so much today from rheumatic pains in my legs.

The snow was deep and thick, and we were flanked by guards and Alsatian dogs on both sides. My biggest worry was how Hela, now a frail invalid, would survive the journey. She was travelling with some people who lived on one of the neighbouring farms and had a horse and wagon. They were under orders from the Nazis to transport supplies to Auschwitz, and we had arranged for them to take Hela with them.

Mother and I went into the hospital to fetch her. We propped her up between us and helped her into the wagon, which was waiting outside the hospital gate.

Then we went to join our group. We started walking, several thousands of us: the women in front, the men behind. The snow was falling heavily, and the roads were icy. There was no food, and we had to eat the snow, which was dirty from the boots of all the people who had walked that way before us.

In the early mornings, the snow was hard and crisp, but it soon turned to slush from so many pairs of feet marching. I could feel the vibrations from my boots as they squelched along.

We were longing for a drop of water. People all around me were slipping and sliding, perspiring from weakness and lack of nourishment, dropping like flies. The guards were shooting them into the gutters.

Every few miles they shouted: '*Halt!*' We had to stop and be counted to check whether anyone had escaped. We marched in rows of ten, and if anyone in a row went missing, every tenth person was shot. Each of us, therefore, had a responsibility to look after our neighbours. One would have thought that, because of the sheer numbers of people marching, some guards might have overlooked the occasional escape attempt, but they all acted with the typical military mentality of the SS regime. They even counted the numbers of the dead.

There was always a distance, a barrier between them and us. We were the 'displaced persons'; they were the *Herrenvolk*, the superior race.

As we walked, we passed the bodies of men who had been shot from the previous transport. Their bodies had rolled down into the gutters. We saw the men lying there in their striped jackets and trousers, some of them still wearing their Jewish flat caps.

Non-Jewish people had also been shot: among them, Polish political prisoners with the letter 'P' daubed on their backs.

The guards were meticulously observant, watching to see if anyone made a false move. If we fell, we had no chance. However tired or drained we felt, we had to keep moving and stay upright. Whenever we saw a guard looking at us, we straightened our shoulders to show that we were still fit.

Having seen Hela safely on to the wagon, I now concentrated on my mother. I tried to keep her spirits up so that she wouldn't lose hope. When she showed signs of flagging, I lifted her up underneath her arms and we walked quite fast so that the guards wouldn't notice she was losing strength. She said to me: 'I can't.' 'Come on,' I said. 'They are watching. Show that you can walk properly.' And together we walked strong, straight and steady.

My leg was still septic and extremely painful from the dog bites I received at Plaszov. Despite regular applications of salted water, the wound was slow to heal and in danger of turning gangrenous. I kept quiet about it, because life had to go on and the Nazis were only interested in the strongest and the fittest.

I tried not to let the fatigue and discomfort of the long trek prey on my mind. The mental anguish of walking into an uncertain future far outweighed the physical pain in my legs and body.

Whenever we had the chance to sit down, we discarded some of our belongings, digging them into the snow to make a lighter load.

The guards allowed us the occasional rest, because they were tired as well, but their rest was different from ours. They rested in warm clothes, fortified by food and drink. We were sparsely dressed, starving and thirsty.

We walked all day long for about three weeks, spending the nights in villages, sleeping on the snow in fields and farms. The guards would take over an entire village and surround it. They would watch us from strategic positions. People slept wherever they could find a spare piece of ground: in a farmhouse or a barn, or out in the open.

Many of the villagers were frightened and stayed in their houses as we passed by. We could see them at their windows staring out at us.

In one village Mother and I slept on the hay in a stable. The wind was howling and making the snow drift in through the roof and under the walls. I was lying there shivering with my mother next to me when I felt a hard object beneath me. I pulled and tugged at the hay and eventually found a small parcel. When I unwrapped it I discovered a pair of elasticated long-johns: large, white and fringed with lace. They had been left in the hay, perhaps as an act of compassion, by the people who lived at that particular farm. Whatever the reason, I was glad that I found them. For me, it was a miracle. In those frosty nights, any extra layer of warmth for the body was more than welcome, and I put them on over my pair of silk stockings and my thin pair of knickers.

A couple of nights later, my mother and I slept on a pile of logs in a farmyard. The logs were stacked on a kind of cart, and we had to climb up on to them from the snow. We curled up together, covering ourselves with our coats, my mother's feet turned towards my face and my feet to my mother's face.

We fell asleep from sheer exhaustion. When I woke up, the clear, bright moon was shining down on to the snow, giving it a glossy white sheen. It must have been about midnight. When I tried to get up I was so stiff with cold that at first my legs would not budge. They felt like solid lumps of wood, and I had to lift one leg at a time, flexing the muscles until they slowly came to life again.

I stepped down on to the snow. I felt so disorientated that my mind was barely functioning, and my circulation must have almost stopped. If I had lain there any longer I am sure I would have frozen to death.

I quickly woke my mother and told her to get up. I could see the light from a farmer's cottage several yards away. The guards were stationed close by, with their dogs, but I was past caring whether they saw me and pointed their guns at me. I was beyond feeling, or worrying about what became of me. I do not think that, at that point, food plays such a big part as warmth in the struggle to survive.

The farmer's cottage was about 300 metres away, and it took me some time to crawl there. Its light was reflecting on to the snow in the moonlight. The guards continued sleeping, and the dogs stayed quiet.

I knocked on the front door; someone opened it and I went in. I noticed several people from the march sitting on the stairs in the dark. To have already discovered such a cosy refuge, they had obviously been cleverer than I had!

An elderly man and his wife appeared, and they had a little girl with them. They were Germans of Polish descent. In their living room there was a low, round oven full of logs which gave out a strong heat.

I asked them if I could bring my 'friend'. The splitting up of families had started in Plaszov, and I had to be careful not to reveal that we were mother and daughter. I therefore learned to think of my mother as a 'friend'. We walked as strangers, anonymously, with our numbers on our backs.

The couple said I could bring my 'friend' and I went back to the farmyard to fetch her. We reached the cottage and Mother staggered into the hall, so exhausted that she could scarcely stand. She sat on the stairs with the other people from the march, and the farmer gave us some hot black coffee, which tasted wonderful. Then we wound our way through the crowds sitting and standing in the long corridor, and into the living room. We sat around the fire and warmed ourselves.

The farmer and his wife helped to pull off my boots, which were soaked through with water. I hung up my long-johns on a line to dry, and the farmer's wife gave me a clean pair of socks to put on. We drank our coffee, slowly dried our feet and began to feel human again.

Some of the guards were under the same roof as us, playing cards in another room close by and unaware of what was going on elsewhere in the cottage.

When I saw that glowing oven, I was reminded of a strange dream that I'd had the night before we left Plaszov. It was almost like a premonition. I dreamed that after a terrible journey tramping through heavy mud for miles, I woke up in a beautifully clean bed in a light, warm room next to a hot, wrought-iron stove. In reality, I dozed off briefly on the stairs with my fellow travellers.

We couldn't stay long at the cottage, as we had to move on. As we were leaving, the farmer and his wife gave Mother and me a large tin of conserved meat which they had already opened for us. The woman in particular seemed nervous about doing this, and I suppose the Nazis could have implicated them for associating with us, but that tin of meat really helped us to survive. It was the first proper food – and the last – we had to sustain us throughout our long, arduous journey. Mother and I shared it around in tiny helpings, each of us nibbling a piece or just wetting our mouths with it, enjoying the flavour. It was a wonderful source of nourishment for many women on that journey.

If I could trace our host and hostess at the farm I would love to go back and say 'Thank you'. The few hours we spent in the shelter of their home was a rare period of peace for us during our trek through Poland.

We must have been walking for about three weeks and it snowed all the way. Sometimes we were made to walk overnight. We kept wondering: 'When will it end? How much further?'

As we got nearer to Auschwitz and the German border, some people came out of their houses with buckets of water and deliberately poured it on the ground in front of us, to mock us. Some stood eating chunks of bread as they watched us pass by.

But only a minority acted in that way. We experienced compassion and humanity, too: the parcel of long-johns in the stable; the hot coffee and the tin of meat. Incidents like this gave us faith that there is some goodness in people.

The first sight that greeted us as we walked through the massive iron gates into the muddy compound at Auschwitz was a small group of women fiddlers. They came out of a hut on our left-hand side, playing their instruments. I remember thinking: 'This is like a madhouse.' It was too sweet, too good. I was suspicious, because I felt that the sweetness of the music was likely to signify a brutal act. It seemed ominous. I recalled the woman violinist at Plaszov playing and singing while the girl was dragged round the square by her hair.

We learned later that it was standard procedure for these musicians to play for the incoming transports on their way to the gas chamber.

As soon as we arrived we were segregated. The guards there told us that we were going to the shower room and that our clothes would be disinfected. We undressed and left our clothes in a heap on a bench outside. They shouted at us: 'Go in! Quick!' And they locked the doors behind us.

There must have been about a hundred of us squashed into the stone-walled room, with no windows and narrow openings in the ceiling. We stood there for an hour or so, and nothing happened. The waiting seemed endless. Nobody spoke. After the gruelling journey everybody felt too dejected and exhausted to talk, and yet the fear of what might happen to us was still very strong.

Suddenly the huge metal doors opened and a tall woman with a thin face rushed in. I recognised her at once. She had been a clerk in one of the offices at Plaszov and I had spoken to her once or twice before. I was standing close to the doors and she noticed me immediately. She said: '*You* are here?' She was astonished to see me.

She then ran through another door and I didn't see her again. About ten minutes later, water began pouring down from the ceiling. We showered ourselves, enjoying the feeling of the fresh, cool water on our tired, aching bodies.

When the doors opened again and we got out, several other women embraced us. Some were civilians, DPs (displaced persons) like ourselves, whom the Nazis had recruited to work there. They said to us: 'Do you realise you've escaped the furnace?' I opened my eyes very wide and said: 'Furnace? What furnace?' 'The gas chamber,' they said.

It had not dawned on me that this was where we had been sent. We went in there, not knowing what would happen, wondering. We were standing there naked, and our clothes had been destroyed. After we had gone in, those women never expected to see us again. 'How is it possible?' they said. If they hadn't told us, we would have been none the wiser.

We all wept tears of joy. I shall never know how we came out alive. The gas chamber was operated from another part of the camp. Had the gas supply suddenly failed? Why did the guards, usually so super-efficient, fail to discover this and not send us back inside again? Was the woman I knew an angel from heaven or some higher power, who had appeared through those heavy iron doors to save us from death?

The same procedure must have taken place with people from previous transports. They, too, must have stripped and had their clothes destroyed but, unlike us, they never came out again.

We were given yellow-striped coats and dresses and taken to the main annexe at Birkenau, about two miles away. The long wooden barracks where we slept were overcrowded, unheated, filthy, dingy. The stone floors were so damp that, for added protection, my mother used to tie old pieces of rag around her shoes.

In the middle of each barrack was a distempered stove that was supposed to heat the whole barrack. Everybody used to gather around this stove, trying to get warm, but most of the time it was ice-cold and not functioning efficiently.

We soon realised that, in comparison with Auschwitz, Plaszov had been a paradise. There at least we could be sure of a regular ration of bread and soup, a change of clothes and washing facilities. We had become accustomed to a certain routine: the five a.m. count and roll-call in the main square, where we waited until Commandant Goeth arrived and gave us the all-clear to go to work. We had come to know the danger signs. We knew, when Goeth wore his green pointed hat and swaggered around the camp with his dogs, that a mass shooting was imminent.

At Auschwitz we had no idea what to expect, which way to turn. The water was undrinkable and we lived mainly on beet soup, but there were no set days when the ration would be distributed. The fear was even greater than before, because now it was fear of the unknown. We were surrounded by different sets of *kapos*, different inmates, unfamiliar faces that stared at us in a hostile way. The whole system here was alien and we felt very isolated. Our neighbouring inmates included about half a dozen women from Plaszov, among them Sali Silberling, a Czech girl who had been put in charge of the main clothing store at Plaszov. Sali and I were together throughout the long walk to Auschwitz. She used to keep some money nailed into the heels of her shoes, and the Nazis never discovered this.

The fear did not lessen with time. At night we would drop off to sleep, then wake up in a cold sweat, frightened that somebody might burst in and punish us for the slightest misdemeanour. We had to stay alert all the time.

People were crippled, trussed up and lashed. It was the same scenario as at Plaszov, but the conditions were even more degrading. I shall never forget the terror in people's eyes.

We knew that Auschwitz was the end of the road. Tens of thousands of people had been here before us, and most had ended up in the gas chamber. We used to hear transports coming and going day and night, and we saw people being loaded on to trucks. In one incident I saw a truck full of children arriving. They had no chance at all and were dumped straight into the ovens.

Bodies were burned fast, and wherever we went the awful stench from the crematorium followed us. It was the most shocking, acrid smell, and it will always stay with me.

At Auschwitz, every last remnant of respect and dignity was squeezed out of us. In our loose, striped, insect-ridden clothing and with our hair cropped or shaved, we felt completely dehumanised.

Every morning we got dressed and stood by our bunks while the *blockowa* counted us. If anyone went missing it was the usual procedure: every tenth person was singled out and shot.

We were not allowed to go outside the barrack, unless we were allocated a job for that day. The *blockowa* would call out various

names: 'So-and-so is wanted *here . . . there . . .*' A guard escorted
us to and from work. No one was allowed to go out of the camp
to work.

Some of us had regular jobs. The luckier ones worked in the
kitchens; others had to scrub the floors or – the most unpopular
job of all – the toilets. The latrine block was like the one at
Plaszov: primitive and extremely public, with permanent queues.
No such thing as flush toilets!

There were rats in the latrines in both camps, but they were
considered a minor inconvenience.

No cleaning materials were available and we had to clean those
lavatories with our bare hands. Afterwards, we smuggled some
cold water back to the barrack, if possible, and kept washing our
hands over and over again. There were a few cold water taps in
the camp, but they were not easily accessible in the ice and snow.
Besides, our morale was so low that we even became scared to be
seen washing ourselves in case this was regarded as a punishable
offence.

At the end of each day, the *blockowa* sounded a whistle, the
signal to stop work and return to our barracks. Our hours varied,
but they were always long, and we were usually so exhausted
that we could hardly summon up the energy to stand and be
counted.

The restrictions were so great that if we wanted to go to the
lavatory in the night we would have to choose a moment when
the searchlights were not shining on us. One day we had to walk
to the latrine block naked with our arms stretched out in front of
us, to show that we were not concealing anything on our bodies.
As if we were robbers. I had to sacrifice my last possession of any
real meaning or value: a silver signet ring, a gift from my mother
which I had somehow managed to keep hidden at Plaszov.

Because of the squalid conditions and deficient diet in the
ghetto and the camps, my periods had gradually disappeared, and
I never experienced a normal menstrual flow. At Auschwitz they
stopped completely, and did not recommence until after we

were liberated. Sanitary towels, of course, were non-existent and women had to manage by tearing off odd pieces of clothing to use as protection, washing and re-cycling them.

Everyone was fighting for their own existence. We were afraid to get too involved in any discussions, especially about political affairs, because there was no way of being sure who was an enemy and who was a friend. We had to be discreet in our dealings with people, in case what we said got back to the *blockowa* and she reported to the *kapo*.

We were at Auschwitz for under a month, so there was little time to get acquainted with the regime. Soon after we arrived, I enquired about Hela. The Polish *blockowa* in our block had a few girls working for her, helping to distribute the soup and bread. Unlike the rest of us, these helpers had permission to move freely between barracks. I happened to know one of them from Plaszov. She told me that Hela had arrived safely and had been taken straight to the hospital there. I could hardly believe it, as I never thought she would survive the journey.

The girl offered to take me to see Hela. If we wanted anything, we had to make use of many different people. One person would ask another, and so on, through the camp grapevine.

She smuggled me through the barracks, away from the eyes of the guards and *kapos*. It was so quiet during the day that you could have heard a pin drop.

We sneaked our way into the hospital, a large barrack with a stone floor and so dark that I could hardly see across the room. It was the most horrifying scene: so many people – old, young, all herded together helplessly in bunks along the walls and in the centre of the barrack.

I guessed that most of the patients were probably victims of experiments, guinea pigs for the Nazis' élite medical teams. The young girls aged quickly, they looked like old women: haggard and wrinkled long before their time.

I could see Hela on the opposite side of the barrack. She saw me and called me over. I had never cried in front of her before, but knowing how desperately ill she was I couldn't hold back the tears.

She said: 'Don't cry. I will be all right. If you want to stay here a while, I will hide you under my bed covers – and tell Mother to come here too.' But there were rumours that the camp was mined and we would have to leave. I couldn't tell my sister this, so I simply said: 'I will ask Mother if she will come.'

I don't know if she realised what was going on or how sick she was. Dr Schindler from Plaszov was in charge of the patients, but he said he could do nothing more for Hela. Like most of the other patients, she was now beyond help. He was powerless to stop these barbaric experiments and the hospital lacked even the most basic medicines to relieve some of the worst symptoms. Other SS 'medical' teams used to come in from outside the camps and it was they who selected various inmates to be experimented on. The notorious pioneer of these experiments was Dr Josef Mengele, the camp commandant. I once caught sight of him in the distance, but I do not recall his looks very clearly. We inmates had to make ourselves invisible and it was not done to stare at anybody for long. We dared not even talk about Mengele – or any other SS official – among ourselves, for fear of betrayal. Instead, we expressed our fears and anxieties with our eyes, not with words.

My visit to the hospital had to be brief, a few minutes at the most, in case I was stopped and questioned. Fortunately, there were no guards in the hospital barrack.

Soon, we had to get ready to march away from the camp, as there were plans to liquidate it – for the same reasons as at Plaszov. Increasing numbers of Nazis were needed at the Front. We suspected that the German Army must be in retreat, though we did not realise that the war was in its final stages.

When we were a few feet from the hospital gate I sneaked in there to say goodbye to Hela. She begged me to stay, but Mother was waiting outside for me in the road and I had to take up my position next to her, ready to be counted.

Hela gave me her ration of bread as I was leaving. It was the last time I ever saw her. I said to Mother: 'Hela wants to see you. Will you go?' She went in. I thought she might have decided to stay with Hela, but after a few minutes I saw her running back. She wanted to come with me. It must have been an agonising moment for her, but it was entirely her decision and I had said nothing to influence her.

When she returned, there was already movement outside: bustle, barked commands, loudspeakers calling this block and that block. We had to check quickly which was our group and line up in tens. As we walked through the gates, the guards were assembled on either side to escort us.

The Nazis' decision to move us on again after less than one month in Auschwitz meant that Mother and I succeeded in avoiding the tattooing ritual. Many of the inmates had been there much longer than us and had been tattooed on their arms on first entering the camp. Shortly before we marched off, we heard rumours that the Nazis were planning to start tattooing people's foreheads, but in the end they had no time to do this. Consequently, this was yet another lucky escape for my mother and me.

7

Not Enough Ink...

We left Auschwitz in January 1945 for an unknown destination. We marched in the middle of main roads, through built-up areas and villages, accompanied by the familiar battalions of SS guards and Alsatian dogs on both sides of us. Thousands of us were marching, in a long trail, through the deep, dirty snow. We walked ten abreast, changing to four abreast when the road narrowed. The queue straggled out of line as more and more people dropped away from exhaustion. The guards were counting us all the time. Numbers were an obsession with them. They were worried that someone might escape and spread the news about their brutal treatment of us, but where could we escape to? No one dared even try.

At Auschwitz the SS had opened up the main food store and given us each some bread for the journey, but this was a mixed blessing. Hela had given us her ration, a round black loaf, and our bags were already too heavy to cope with even these small extra items. Mother and I began by carrying the loaves between us wrapped in a thick scarf. We nibbled bits of bread along the way, but when we stopped for a rest we pushed the remainder underneath the snow. Others did the same. People were far too weak to carry them, though anyone could have been shot for shedding their load in this way.

We were gasping for a drink. We felt dried up. We begged for water from passers-by but nobody gave us any. Once again, we were forced to witness the cruel spectacle of residents coming out of their houses with buckets full of water and emptying them on the snow in front of us.

I wondered how people could be so unkind. Was this normal human behaviour? It made me feel like an outcast.

After we had disposed of our bread, we had no food left and, for a second time, had to resort to eating the snow.

As we were walking through one village, two Polish girls came up to me and stuffed four cigarettes into my hand. I was terrified that they would be shot for this generous gesture and I whispered to them: 'Please go away, or you will get caught.' Those cigarettes made us feel like millionaires. We couldn't smoke them right away, but when we were allowed to stop and rest I shared them with some friends. I was very touched and felt that some people at least were in sympathy with us and had not been corrupted by anti-Jewish propaganda.

We marched and marched, deep into Germany. After several days we came to Leslau, a small town with a railway station, where we were loaded on to long, high, open trucks. Anyone who refused to go – and there were some – was immediately shot by the guards.

The train gradually started filling up. The guards were standing beside the trucks, and while they were facing the other way I managed to climb down on to the wheels and sneak along the side of the train to collect some water from the engine. Fortunately, my truck was right next to the engine, and the driver was not a Nazi.

I crept back again with my meat tin filled with water, and pulled myself up into the truck by the handles on the side. My mother and I drank the water. We were so desperately thirsty that we didn't mind the smell of paraffin. It was wet and fluid and that was all that mattered to us.

Sometimes, when I lie in bed today and think about the risks I took, I wonder how I did it. I took my life in my hands. It shows how one loses one's fear in certain situations; one is forced to act in order to survive.

We were horribly cramped in those trucks. We sat on the floor like heaps of cabbages, our knees up against our chins. It was absolutely freezing. The snow drifted into the trucks and down on to our shoulders, and we were brushing it away and clinging to each other to keep warm.

Hundreds died on the journey. When we stopped at some stations in the country, we had to throw the bodies out into the fields. The Nazis did nothing. They only gave orders. They wanted, as always, to degrade us. The lifting up and disposing of corpses – mothers, fathers, older children – were left to the inmates.

We travelled in these confined conditions for three or four weeks. Sometimes the train stopped in sidings or stations in the middle of nowhere. We discovered later that this was to give priority to military convoys.

The guards used to get down from the trucks and hang around in groups, smoking and talking. At some of the bigger stations we saw crowds of people waiting on the platforms: German civilians, with a lot of luggage. They were rushing here and there with their cases. There was an atmosphere of tension. We felt that something was up. We smelled it.

One night, we found ourselves in Buchenwald camp, which was a men's camp near Weimar. As at Plaszov and Auschwitz, the railway line came right into the camp. It was pitch dark and the guards were wandering around outside with torches.

First, we unloaded the dead bodies. Then we were ordered down from the trucks and told to stand in a queue. The prisoners there took pity on us and gave up their soup for us. We must have looked ravenous. The men themselves looked drawn and they were shivering from the cold, muffled up in coats and scarves. I could see the barracks in the distance.

As we queued, we could smell the aroma of the soup and see the steam pouring out of large metal urns. It was the most beautiful soup I have ever tasted: barley, potatoes and herbs. With all the ingredients that one can obtain today, I don't think it would be possible to produce such delicious soup.

There were no proper dishes or plates, but everybody had some sort of container. All I had was the small, empty meat tin. After a long wait I filled it up with the soup and gave it to my mother, but she rushed away and drank it so quickly that I had to rejoin the queue and wait for another helping for myself. The taste of that soup remains vividly in my mind because of those men who sacrificed their ration.

While we were waiting, one young man aged about 20 walked past and whispered to me in Polish: 'Head up. Don't lose hope. It won't be long now: the war is ending.' Those few warm, human words gave me quite a boost. It was the first real news from outside we had had for over four years.

After we finished drinking the soup, we sat around the camp compound for a while. A few hours later, we had to go to the opposite side of the station where we were loaded on to closed-in trucks. We helped each other up into the trucks, climbing on to a pair of shoulders, lifting and pulling one person after another. There were no steps and no footholds. Everything had to be accomplished with speed. There were the usual cold, brusque, impatient shouts of the guards: '*Schnell! Schnell!*'

There were sliding doors all along the side of the train. When we were all inside, we heard 'click click' sounds as the cattle trucks were sealed off from the outside.

It was an extremely long train and absolutely packed. Each truck had a tiny opening for a window, about a foot square and situated very high up. There were about a hundred of us crouched on the floor of each truck. We had no food, no air, no toilet facilities. All the time one was aware of a persistent, putrid smell, a suffocating stuffiness.

Conditions were so appalling that people's bodily functions were affected and they felt completely blocked inside, unable to pass any water or motion. If you wanted to, you just held it back, which may be why I have a defective kidney today.

At other times, we used that meat tin and washed it out whenever we could.

We were resigned to what might be done to us. We thought: 'The end must come any day. We are going to be destroyed. They want us here? – we go here. They want us there? – we go there.' But somehow, despite it all, I kept remembering that young Polish man at Buchenwald and his words of hope.

We were stuck inside those trucks for many days and weeks. It seemed more like years. The train stopped at certain stations but we couldn't get out and we couldn't see where we were. There were so many people in each truck that it was impossible to get near the window to see out.

People spent the time dozing, then waking up, then drifting back into sleep again from a combination of hunger and lack of oxygen. Sometimes I had to get up and stretch my legs and toes, to stop myself seizing up with cramp.

Tensions were running so high that even the smallest incident jarred our nerves. I remember two sisters in their early twenties sitting next to me, who started to argue for no apparent reason. My mother asked them what they were quarrelling about. One of them became hysterical and shouted at my mother: 'It has got nothing to do with you.'

Then the two girls started to fight. Tempers flared up. We tried to pull them apart, my mother and I, and someone else on the other side of them joined in. They hit and scratched us and tore the hood off my coat, but after all we'd been through this was of minor importance. We felt pain, but what's a bit of pain?

Things quietened down eventually. The trucks stopped and we heard the usual coarse voices of the guards: *'Raus! 'Raus!'* We clambered down the sides of the trucks into some woods. It was very dark and the only light came from the reflection of the gleaming white of the snow on the ground.

My first thought, as we lined up to be counted for the umpteenth time, was that they might decide to shoot us all, as they had shot many thousands before us in similar woodland terrain. Instead, they made us march through the woods in thick snow, for several hours, until we arrived at Bergen-Belsen.

It was February 1945 and we entered the camp through heavy, soggy snow-covered mud. The camp was a wild, open complex surrounded by searchlights and barbed wire, a huge expanse of long, shell-like barracks with openings for windows. We were packed into these barracks like sardines, one on top of the other. Some barracks had bunks, but there were none in mine, just bare wooden floors and a dim light bulb in the ceiling.

Mother and I collapsed into a corner, hot and tired from the walking. In the morning, when daylight broke, I saw people wandering about outside. They looked thin and emaciated, starved and disease-ridden. I noticed three of these walking skeletons coming towards me, their eyes bulging out of their sockets. I thought: 'They have sent us here so that we will end up looking the same way.' This was such a terrifying prospect that instinct took over and I told myself: 'I'm *not* going to get to that stage.' I shook myself, got up and walked out of the barrack, stepping over the piles of people lying there.

Outside, bodies were everywhere. Chaos. People from every barrack looking to see if they could find any relations still alive. The barracks were sandwiched close together and it was easy to lose oneself in the crowd. The guards were stationed in their control towers around the edge of the camp, but there were fewer of them on the ground than in previous camps. So I, too, began to look around in the hope of coming across any remaining members of my family: a distant relative, perhaps.

I could see nobody I knew, and after a while I found myself in a hospital barrack. It was a small short-stay cottage hospital, where the Wehrmacht (Army) were sent before being transferred to the main hospital outside Belsen.

I knew some people who worked there. They had been with me at Auschwitz. One was a Polish secretary, short and dark, but whose name I don't remember. I asked her if I could help in any way, and she told me to come back the following morning.

I had always had a flair for nursing. It had been my ambition to study medicine until the war came along and destroyed my

ABOVE LEFT: This photograph of me was taken in Hanover, Germany, in September 1945.

ABOVE RIGHT: Norman on his call-up in 1940, when he joined the Royal Artillery Searchlights.

LEFT: September 1945: Norman and I together in Germany ten days before our wedding.

BELOW LEFT: With 'Lulu' McKitrick, Norman's great friend and fellow sergeant who made all the arrangements for our wedding (including getting hold of a British silk parachute, from which my wedding dress was made).

ABOVE: The wedding photograph. Apart from myself, there are only three other women present. I felt sad that, because the journey would have been too strenuous for her, my mother could not be with us.

RIGHT: Arriving in England, 10 November 1945. A crowd of photographers and reporters awaited 'the bride from Belsen'.

OPPOSITE ABOVE: After the wedding, we had a reception at 53 Field Security HQ near Plön. I was too full of emotion to eat much!

OPPOSITE BELOW: The marriage ceremony on 7 October 1945 at a synagogue in Lübeck which the Germans had used as a stable during the war. Ours was the first post-war wedding to take place there. Norman's commanding officer, Captain Keith Stephen (standing behind Norman), gave me away; Rabbi Leslie Hardman married us.

ABOVE: Norman and I in April 1985, on the eve of returning to Belsen for the 40th anniversary of the liberation.

BELOW: Rogues' gallery. The man I am pointing to is Josef Kramer, camp commandant at Belsen.

dreams. Here was an opportunity for me to learn more, even if it was hardly in ideal circumstances. I had read up a lot about medical issues before the war, both from books and first-aid lessons. In the shelters we learned what to do in an emergency – for instance, if a person was wounded in the street.

So I talked my way into a job at the hospital. I brought Tola with me the next morning. She was in my barrack. She was a pretty, blonde girl of about my age. We met at Auschwitz, where she had helped our *blockowa* unload and distribute the ration of bread from the main food store.

It was a short walk from the living quarters to the hospital. At the gate Irma Grese, head of the *Aufseherinnen* (Nazi women leaders), and her colleagues, dressed in their blue-grey uniforms and boots, searched us thoroughly. My mother had given me part of her bread ration and I slipped it into my bag. Irma Grese unzipped the bag, discovered the piece of bread and lashed out at me, slapping me on both sides of my face. It was like being slashed by a knife.

She snatched my bag away from me and tossed it into a heap of other people's belongings. Underneath the lining of my bag was a picture of my sister, Miriam. I didn't mind about losing the bread, but that photograph meant the world to me.

She was tall and had the strength of a strong man – so much so that when she hit me I almost fell. You could tell, from her mannerisms and demeanour, that she was unmistakably in charge. She was very good-looking and often changed her hairstyle. Her hair was usually drawn back from her face, and sometimes she wore it in ringlets. But her face always showed hatred and contempt.

Every morning she searched us. Very rarely could a group of us walk past without someone being hit or kicked. We might drop something, out of sheer fright, and one of the *Aufseherinnen* would say: 'Pick this up,' or 'You dropped that.' While we were bending down to pick up the object in question they would kick us or punch us, always with a sarcastic laugh. They were constantly

looking for ways of catching us out. We just had to pretend not
to notice.

We were lucky to get work in the hospital, because it meant
that we could scrounge left-overs from the patients' meals and
take them back to the camp for my mother and some friends:
soup, or an extra piece of bread.

Our only ration, about twice a week, was a small crust of stale
black bread, so hard that we could hardly bite into it. We were
also given soup, which had been doctored with ground glass.
After Liberation, the British soldiers found sacks of this glass in
the kitchens. Many of the inmates died because the glass ripped
open their insides. Others suffered from diarrhoea, dysentery and
other diseases.

On Mondays the patients had a very thick soup of bacon,
sausage and ham. On our first day Tola and I managed to put
aside a ladle of this soup. We poured it into a bottle and smuggled
it back to the barrack (in the evenings the *Aufseherinnen* were less
scrupulous about searching us). We also found two slices of bread
and shared them out: one to my mother, the other to friends.

I came across a few girls I knew from Cracow. One was Sali
Silberling, the Czech girl who had walked with me from Plaszov
to Auschwitz. Her brother in England tried to contact her at
Belsen through the Red Cross so that she could become a
naturalised British subject. Unfortunately, she never got that far.
After a few days in Belsen she and some of the other girls were
sent away on a transport. We never heard of any of them again.

I met up again with Karola, my friend at Plaszov, with whom
I had celebrated the fast the previous October. She was working
in one of the kitchens at Belsen and one day she gave me a piece
of meat. It was tough and unappetising and needed a lot of
chewing, but she marched me up and down the room until I
swallowed it. She wanted me alone to have it because she knew
that whatever I had I would share and she felt I was the one who
needed it most.

Karola's sister-in-law was also doing kitchen work. They had not seen each other since the sister-in-law had been sent away on a transport many months previously from Plaszov.

I got to know some new Polish inmates, among them Maria, a non-Jewish nurse who worked with me at the hospital.

The patients ate little. They were mostly wounded soldiers and were not there for long before moving on to the main hospital in Bergen, near Celle.

On one occasion I managed to find a few cigarette stumps in an ashtray in one of the two wards. I attached them to a hair slide and later, back at the barrack, several of us had a puff. We regarded this as the most fantastic treat and enjoyed it so much that we didn't stop to consider the risks we might be taking from such illicit nourishment. For all we knew, the soldiers might have had TB or some other infectious condition.

Tola and I carried out the routine nursing duties: washing patients, emptying bed pans, making beds, handing out pills and meals. The food arrived every morning from the Wehrmacht headquarters. We had the use of a little ante-room with bath, toilet, table, kettle, disinfectant and other cleaning materials.

I sometimes used to meet my secretary friend there, but we had to be very discreet. Talking was taboo, and even if we knew someone well, we were frightened to be too open with them, because everybody was under pressure from the SS. If the guards noticed two people chatting together, they would beat them up or set the dogs on them. So there was little conversation among inmates and most people became very introspective.

Many of the SS personnel who had been at Auschwitz moved on to Belsen: Mengele, Josef Kramer (camp commandant at Belsen) and Dr Klein, who was in charge of the hospital. Klein used to come in every morning, check that everything was in order and go off to the other hospital in the afternoon. He never spoke much and we didn't exchange any words. He had a small team of helpers, including a Nazi dentist and his Jewish-Czech assistant. The assistant and his wife were a peculiar couple. She often used to come into the little bathroom to wash herself but she never spoke and it was impossible to communicate with either of them.

An epidemic of typhus was sweeping through the camp. It spread through the lice which lived on people's bodies in the barracks. These lice were everywhere, crawling from bunk to bunk, person to person. Some people had them in their hair, which could be extremely dangerous. My worst experience of lice had been in the uniforms factory, but by the time I reached Belsen my head was completely clear.

One day, soldiers from the Wehrmacht came and queued up to be inoculated, and Tola and I assisted Dr Klein with a mass inoculation programme, mopping up with disinfectant and cotton wool. A couple of days after the main influx of Wehrmacht, two soldiers walked in and begged me to inject them. It was in the afternoon and all the doctors had gone to the main hospital, so I told the two men I had no authority to do this. I was scared and thought they might be trying to trick me. Puzzled, too: why had they missed the original queue?

They told me they were frightened about being infected, and assured me they were Wehrmacht, not SS, but had been unable to come before with their unit. I was concerned about what might happen to me afterwards, as I was unsupervised. If word had got back to Dr Klein, I could have been shot. But they said they would take the responsibility, so I injected them and off they went.

Fortunately, there were no repercussions, but I wouldn't dare do this today without a doctor's advice or instructions.

Another afternoon, while Dr Klein and his team were in the other hospital, I gave myself a typhus injection. I also managed to smuggle a few kohl (charcoal) tablets back to the barrack in the evenings for my mother, to protect her against dysentery.

One day, when the waiting room was full of patients, Irma Grese came in to collect some tablets. Dr Klein knew the kind of pills she wanted, she had had them before, and I went and got them for her so she was able to jump the queue. She never acknowledged me or said thank you.

Because they were in their sick beds, you would think the patients might have shown some humility, but they treated us in a very superior way, ordering us about as if we were dirt. I spoke to them in German, but there was no real conversation between us.

Their attitude didn't bother me as I was so relieved to have found a job and to be away from the filthy, foul-smelling barrack. It meant that I stood a better chance of surviving. Those who didn't work deteriorated day by day, mentally and physically. The regime at Auschwitz and, especially, Plaszov, had been more organised and there was more for the inmates to do. Belsen was bigger than the other two camps but there were fewer jobs to occupy people.

Some of the inmates were taken outside the camp to clean the soldiers' barracks, which were about two miles away. My mother peeled potatoes in one of the camp's kitchens, a job she acquired through Karola's sister-in-law. Most people wanted to work in the kitchens, because it was warmer and they could grab a bite to eat there. Mother was lucky. Peeling potatoes was considered a high-ranking occupation, a form of promotion.

Before that, she used to peel sugar beets, which were heavy to handle and icy cold from the frost. When she was peeling the beets or potatoes, she had to swathe her hands with old rags to protect them from frostbite, leaving only the tips of her fingers free.

The potatoes went to the guardswomen, but my mother and I sometimes cooked and ate the peel. This was not allowed. If the SS had found even a trace of peel in our pockets we could have been shot.

These days, roughage is supposed to be good for you, but I personally don't care for it. I like my vegetables cooked well, otherwise it reminds me too much of that time when hunger drove us to eat the potato peel.

Mother and I used to get up at four in the morning, to avoid the queues of people waiting to use the shower block about an hour later. We undressed and showered our bodies with ice-cold water. The only soap we had was a barrel of honey-coloured liquid soap, manufactured out of human flesh from the bodies of people shot by the SS on the transports. Many times we wondered: 'Could this be my brother, my sister, another relation?'

Afterwards, we put on the same striped clothes, after first shaking out any insects that may have been lurking there. We tried to keep ourselves as clean as possible, examining our clothes for lice, brushing them hard and washing them thoroughly every evening after work. They were very rarely dry by the morning, but we had to wear them. We had no others.

It was bitterly cold and damp at Belsen, and I used to shiver all night. My legs became numb at times and I had to stand up a lot to keep my circulation going.

I managed to find a thin greyish-brown square of material in the hospital and brought it back to the barrack for my mother to use as a bed covering. She treasured it as if it was the most wonderful, expensive blanket. We also found an old bunk some distance away from the barrack, in a field. We carried it back into the barrack and asked Irka, the *blockowa*, if we could use it. She gave her permission and we took it into 'our' corner. For myself, I got a coat from somewhere and both of us lay on some straw which I'd found in a field.

People's rations were often stolen. A few weeks after my mother and I arrived at Belsen, we moved into another block, where there were bunks. We used to put our ration of bread on a shelf above our bunks, hidden from view. We became friendly with a Russian girl who had a lovely clear singing voice. We often heard her singing away in the barrack – sentimental Russian songs. Mother and I always shared our food with her. One night, after the lights went out, she disappeared and when we woke up in the morning our bread was gone. We never saw her again.

At Belsen people finally lost all sense of morality, pride and dignity. They became like animals. When hunger takes over to that extent, nothing else seems to matter.

At all times of the day and night groups of guards came to the barracks. We were often woken up in the night and had to dress quickly, jump down from our bunks and stand to attention. The guards would look around and fire questions at us. The *blockowa* reported back the numbers of people present and how many had died since the previous inspection. It was just another way of wearing us down.

It was sheer willpower that kept me going. Some women stayed behind in the barrack and just lay there on their bunks, too weak and ill to move. There were more Nazi women guards at Belsen than at the previous camps, and they were all sadistic. If an inmate failed to appear at her place of work, these women guards would charge into the barrack, drag her up by her hair and fling her around outside in front of the other inmates.

They had enormous strength. They were whipping and hitting inmates with no mercy, no feeling at all. Each one wanted to show that she could do better. The more torture they inflicted, the faster they rose in the ranks of the SS.

We did not even attempt to talk to them, as both their actions and their looks made it clear that they had no wish to communicate with us.

Reports came into the hospital every morning of the numbers of inmates who had died in the night. On some nights three hundred people died, on others five hundred. If it was a hundred people, we would say, 'Thank God. It's only a hundred.'

In the morning we used to throw the bodies out of the barrack, but sometimes relatives were reluctant to part with them. I remember two sisters and their mother who were in our barrack. One sister died in the night and the others didn't want to part with her body. The shock that people experienced was so severe that they were in a kind of trance. They wanted to believe that the person was not actually dead, only sleeping.

Everywhere it was the same story. Those left behind became

disheartened, melancholic. They had no energy. They stopped washing or attending to personal hygiene. They did nothing except lie in the barracks and let themselves go until they, too, died.

Wherever we walked, we had to climb over heaps of rotting bodies. The crematorium didn't function properly as it couldn't keep up with the pace of death at Belsen, and so the bodies were left to pile up outside in the mud and slush. It is impossible to describe the scene, the stench of death and dysentery. People's insides were cut away by the ground glass in the soup, and they couldn't make it to the lavatories in time. Bodily functions were performed on any spare piece of ground that could be found, and wherever one looked or stepped there were piles of human excrement.

Anne Frank was in my barrack. She was already at Belsen when I arrived and lay a few bunks away from me, dying from typhus. I can remember so clearly my mother telling me about this Dutch girl in the barrack who had apparently written a diary. Other people were talking about it, too, and whispering and 'shushing' because they knew she was dying. She had had to leave the diary behind in Holland.

Soon after we arrived, somebody came and told me that a woman in one of the barracks wanted to see me. She was the sister of my brother-in-law, the one who was shot with my sister Miriam at Plaszov. This woman was delirious, her temperature was sky-high and her body looked as red as a beetroot. She was calling my name and begging to see me. I tried to calm her down. All I could do was offer her a few words of comfort. I told her: 'Hold on and it will pass,' but she was burned up and soon died.

The hospital was strictly for the Germans, and there was no medical help or treatment available for our people. Concentration camp inmates had no rights.

After I had been working at the hospital for several weeks, I noticed that the SS were burning stacks of papers. At the time we thought they were having a general clear-up, but later we realised that they must have been deliberately destroying all the evidence. They probably sensed the Allies were on their way and the camp would be taken over. When the British entered, they found numerous pages missing from record books – pages recording the names of inmates, many of them distinguished men such as consuls and ambassadors.

I longed for pencils and paper. I used to say that when the war ended there would not be enough ink in the world to write down all the events and experiences of those years.

8

Norman's Chapter

I was a sergeant in the 53 Field Security section of the British Intelligence Corps. We had instructions to take over Belsen camp, and on Sunday, 15 April 1945, at 3 p.m. one of our tanks entered the camp and we followed on foot. The scenes which greeted us were like something out of a horror film. People everywhere were dying. In some cases they were so far gone that you couldn't tell whether they were young or old, woman or man.

To survive, they had been reduced to cannibalism. Some of the bodies I saw had parts of the flesh missing. There were pieces cut out of the thigh and, according to some inmates, livers and lungs had been removed and consumed.

As a young soldier who had witnessed the killing of soldiers and animals on many occasions, I found this a shocking experience. I had seen my share of battle casualties – outside Brussels, outside Hamond in Holland, and – when we were stationed near Mill – I remember the sight of shell-shocked soldiers from the Third Infantry Division returning from the battle lines. But to see thousands of innocent people in a camp (or prison, as the Germans used to call it) being starved to death, murdered, poisoned, was beyond belief.

The first person I arrested was Josef Kramer, the Camp Commandant, known as the Beast of Belsen. On the day our unit arrived, I locked Kramer in a huge meat refrigerator set at a low temperature, which the Germans had been using for their own food supplies. I put two guards on him. He was in there for 24 hours before we took him out. Then I interrogated him and made out the arrest warrant.

When I arrested him I said in German: 'I'm a Jew.' He said: 'That's impossible. There are no Jews in the Army. We are killing them all.' I said: 'There are thousands of them in the British Army and the American Army – all freedom-loving people.' But he was still adamant.

I was very proud of being a Jew who arrested one of the most notorious gangsters in Nazi Germany. Maybe it was Fate that a Jew should arrest one of the war's worst concentration camp guards. It was a remarkable moment, but first and foremost I was doing my duty as a soldier, a British soldier, and these were evil men and women who had to be brought to justice.

Kramer was unshaven and very well-fed. He had a faraway look, like a frightened animal that's just been cornered. When I said: '*Look* at these people . . .' he shrugged his shoulders and said: 'We had no medical supplies, and not enough food for ourselves.' I said: 'Look at *you*! You look as if you ate enough for three people.' He kept mumbling to himself: 'I only acted on orders from my superiors.' But he was the camp commandant!

He was a typical bulldog. He was like a robot, and he showed no feeling, no remorse at all. When he was the commandant at Auschwitz he was well known as a murderer and would think nothing of killing up to a hundred people a day himself. This is what I heard from other people I interrogated.

There were lampshades which he had had made in Auschwitz from human skin, and in the kitchens we found bags of ground glass which was used to doctor the inmates' soup.

This was civilisation at its lowest point. It is not humanly possible to believe that anyone can carry out such atrocities and be totally without pity.

There was no opposition from the SS. They gave us no trouble whatsoever. Not one of them tried to fight back, because they were cowards. They only felt themselves brave when they were dealing with unarmed men, women, children and babies. Then they felt superior, but when faced with armies and soldiers they felt small and dejected.

The SS women were the same. They were silent and there was no conversation among them. They looked neither happy nor sad. It was as if they had been drugged.

It was a hot day in April when I arrested them. Over the loudspeaker I called for all SS personnel to line up outside the *Kommandantur* (the former SS headquarters, now taken over by the British Army): the men on one side, the women on the other. I instructed them to lay down their arms and I told them: 'You are all under arrest. You will be tried according to your crimes.'

The inmates were gathered behind them, watching. There was no food about, nothing growing. It was completely bare, not even a blade of grass. Just dust and sand: not nice white desert sand, but grey and arid-looking.

I expected these people to pick up whatever object was to hand and throw it at the SS, but they were quiet. I think many of them had lost all will to live. There was only one incident. A woman aimed a stone at Dr Klein and it hit him in the eye. The soldiers had to hold her back. We had a ring of tanks around the front of the barracks. We thought some of the SS might start making a run for it, but they put down their revolvers and went quietly to be locked in the cells.

We made the SS shift all the bodies into huge pits or craters which were dug by bulldozers. There were thousands of bodies: poor, innocent ex-people, human beings. The SS had to handle them, load the skeletons on to lorries, take the lorries up to the pits and throw the bodies inside. Then the bulldozers filled in this mass grave.

After supervising this for a day or two, our soldiers had become so embittered at what they had seen that, when some of the SS tried to run away, they (the British) emptied their machine guns into them. These boys were so shocked that I think they would have killed any German they had come across.

At first there were 160 SS, but half of them escaped into the forest behind the camp. The agreement with the Wehrmacht was for the Wehrmacht soldiers to go back behind the German lines once the British had taken over the camp, only on condition that the SS remained. The Dutch Resistance fighters who had joined the British Army after Holland had been liberated were waiting for them in the forest and strung them up. The 80 or so SS remaining in the camp knew that the war was over for them.

Some committed suicide. When we put them in the cells we left pieces of rope around and some hanged themselves. They knew they would have no chance, because their crimes were so great.

In my opinion, these were not fit to be called human beings. What isn't always appreciated is that Hitler recruited ex-prisoners – lifers and murderers – to do his dirty work. The first concentration camps, Dachau and Rheinberg, were formed when Hitler came to power in 1933, and the first inmates were political opponents of his regime.

I have been asked why I didn't shoot Kramer right away after witnessing these atrocities, but I had to bear in mind the Werewolves, a German resistance movement formed after Germany was occupied by the Allies. Each town or village in Germany was supposed to have contained a unit which would try to destroy communications and hinder or harass the Allied forces. That was the main reason why we had to be firm and yet diplomatic in order to get information out of them.

After the first day, about a thousand British troops entered Belsen. There were engineers, infantry, tank units, units from every part of the Army. They brought tankers with fresh water, food, clothing, medicines.

As many medical troops as could be spared came, followed by civilian doctors and nurses, bringing blankets and equipment.

We were trying to save lives, but people blamed the British for killing some of the inmates by giving them too much food. This was quite possible. None of us knew what to do until we started getting doctors in. We had no instructions.

We took over a house in Bergen-Belsen as our headquarters. Every time we came into the camp we had to be sprayed with a special powder against typhus. We had all been inoculated against typhus and other diseases; so far as possible we were safe. But on April 18, three days after our arrival, I woke up and could not get out of bed. I was paralysed. That happened to two or three of our chaps. We simply could not walk. When the doctor came and stuck pins in our legs, we felt nothing. This lasted for 24 hours, and they put it down to the shock on our nerves from the horrific sights we'd seen.

For the first few days after the Liberation, a lot of the inmates didn't realise that they were free. They wandered up and down in a daze. I interviewed some Yugoslav and Romanian diplomats. Anyone seeing them would never have imagined they were educated people. They looked like all the others: starved, filthy, disease-ridden. Some had pieces of dirty bread in their hands.

I questioned some of them. I wanted to find out who they were and how they had come to be in the camp.

I remember one morning seeing a man sitting by the gate. He was just bones, and I could see from his features that he was a man, though I couldn't tell his age. He was wearing the yellow striped uniform. He held his hand up, and as I passed he said the Jewish words of a prayer, and then he died.

Another time I saw two sisters. They were looking so pathetic that I called one of them over and gave her my sandwiches, hoping that she would share them with her sister. But she just pushed her sister away and ran off.

There must have been thousands of Germans who knew what was going on, but when we used to ask the German people if they knew about the concentration camps, they would say: 'Yes, we knew, and we were afraid that if we spoke out against the Government, we too would end up in them.' They knew what was going on, but they were only concerned about saving their own skins.

*

On the second day I received information that some SS guards were hiding in the hospital, so a colleague of mine, Harry Bedford, accompanied me there. When we arrived, I saw a dark young woman, who turned out to be a Polish nurse. I said: 'What are you doing here?' When I began to speak, she took fright and ran through a door at the far end of the room. Harry and I stood there, astonished, not knowing what to do.

As we waited, the same door opened and out came a blonde young woman in a white overall. She came over, and I asked her the same question. She couldn't understand, so I spoke in German: 'Who are you? Are you one of the SS?' Most people were wearing torn, dirty clothing, but here was a blonde woman in a clean white overall. She could have belonged to the SS.

'No,' she said. 'I am Polish and Jewish. I've been made a nurse and I took this job to survive.' Then she asked me: 'Are *you* Jewish?' And I said: '*I'm* asking the questions!'

I knew immediately I saw her that we were meant to meet. I'm a very strong believer in Fate. I had come from London, and Gena from Cracow. How would we, in normal circumstances, ever have met? There would have been no chance at all in those days. Today, world travel is a reality, with distance no object, but at that time I certainly would not have gone to Poland, nor Gena to London. Our paths would never have crossed.

In any case, I wasn't supposed to be there at all. I was only there because I'd had to replace a sergeant in our front-line section who was shot in the leg. So Fate definitely played a part in our meeting.

It's the same as when I told my mother the day I joined the Army: 'Don't worry. I shall get through it.' I was so sure that I would come back safely after the war.

So when I first saw Gena I thought: 'This is the girl I am going to marry.' It was as if somebody, some higher power, had told me: 'This is your life partner.'

She looked bloated rather than thin, but there was something

– an indefinable attraction – about her features. In my eyes she looked beautiful.

I knew there might be a delayed reaction to the traumatic events she had suffered, but I wasn't afraid to cope with that. I was there for her to lean on me.

She started telling me about Auschwitz and the other camps. Our unit had not heard of Plaszov camp, and she told me that Kramer had also been the commandant of Auschwitz. We needed evidence for all that. She said to me: 'If you come back tomorrow I will give you details.' We had a German secretary with us, an anti-Nazi and well vetted to do the job. So next day I brought her along and Gena gave her the information.

I felt that I had to go on seeing her. I came back every day and I would bring her some white bread and oranges for her mother.

On the seventh day after the Liberation I asked my commanding officer, Captain Keith Stephen, if I could take Gena to dinner at the Officers' Mess. He said: 'This is very unusual, but I trust you and know the good work you do. You have my permission.'

She arrived with her friend, Tola. My colleagues all rallied around and began congratulating her, and she couldn't understand why. I told her it was our engagement party. She was quite surprised and told me I must have had too much to drink, but I was never a big drinker.

The next day I went to see her and she said: 'You were drunk last night. We are not engaged.' I said: 'Yes, you are my fiancée.' I didn't give her much chance to reject me!

Meanwhile, I carried on with my work and was so busy that Gena and I saw very little of each other. I was fully occupied in the camp and had to leave by eight o'clock each night.

Keith Stephen was a real leader and let everyone in the section use his own initiative. He knew he could rely on his men and he looked after us in a fatherly fashion. After I met Gena, neither he nor my fellow sergeants said anything to discourage or dissuade me. Keith Stephen said: 'You are old enough and you must know what you are doing, and I will help you in every way I can.' And he did.

I was the only sergeant in our unit to have embarked on a romantic relationship at this time. My fellow sergeants all knew that I was determined to go ahead with the marriage and that I had found what I was looking for in my life. It's hard to believe that a love story could materialise from events or circumstances such as these, but, as I said, I'm a fatalist.

I told the Army chaplain, Rabbi Leslie Hardman, that we wished to get married. But the war was still on and I had to leave Belsen on 3 May. I didn't see Gena again until the middle of August.

This was my busiest period for rounding up the top Gestapo, SS and SD (Security Service: the German equivalent to our unit). Our section consisted of one officer, one driver-batman and nine sergeants.

I had been conscripted into the British Army and started my basic training in Taunton at the age of 20. At first I wasn't very keen on the life, but I soon adjusted, and after six weeks' training I joined the Royal Artillery Searchlights near Kidderminster in Worcestershire, in May 1940, as a Bombardier instructing soldiers and ATS (Auxiliary Territorial Service) on aircraft plotting and communications.

After about two years, I was recommended for Officer's training. I was asked to go to Trafalgar House, Charing Cross – in civvies, not in uniform – for an interview. I thought this was in connection with the Officer's training, but when I got there the first thing I saw were posters which read: 'Don't talk. Walls have ears.' I had been chosen to join the Intelligence Corps. On my papers it said that I was a linguist and spoke fluent German. Before the war my father, who was in the fur trade, used to travel on business between London, Paris and Berlin and we spent some years in Germany, where I picked up the language. This was an important factor in my selection.

But I said to the officer at Trafalgar House: 'I don't think I shall be suitable.' My only knowledge of espionage had come from spy movies and I didn't fancy being caught out like some of the characters I'd seen there. I was very young then, just 23, and so I said that I wasn't really interested.

The officer said: 'Well, that means you won't be going back to your unit but into the infantry.' I quickly changed my mind and said: 'Well, I had better volunteer for this, after all.'

He said they would use me for counter-espionage work in the security service.

The training in Wentworth, Surrey, lasted about three months. We had to ride motorcycles and drive lorries, and we had to get to know the workings of pistols and machine guns in case we were called upon to help any troop or unit in trouble.

Then I was taken to do Port Security in Scotland. We had to interview the crew of any liners coming in from neutral countries such as Sweden and find out if any German agents were on board.

From there I went back to my unit at Wentworth where I had 14 days' embarkation leave. I was expecting to leave within a few days for Burma, where I had been given a posting as first reserve, but all 65 soldiers turned up and so I didn't go.

I stayed at Wentworth for another six weeks or so, waiting for another posting. One day, I looked at the notice board in the sergeants' mess and saw that I'd been posted to Highgate, and from there I went to the barracks at Hounslow.

In May 1944, we were posted to Shoreham, in Sussex. There we were told to spread rumours that there were floating anti-aircraft guns in the water (they were actually the floating docks used for the invasion). We were given extra money to go into pubs in the evenings so that we could tell people: 'Oh yes, these are floating ack-ack guns' – in case there were any German agents or fifth columnists around.

On 4 June 1944, we saw the troops on to the boats and knew that the date of the invasion of France was very near.

We landed in France towards the end of June. We did not follow in the wake of advancing troops, because our planned place of work was to be Ostend, so we travelled through France: Bayeux, Caen, through to Abbeville, Lille, moving on to Belgium and bypassing Dehaan, where the Germans held on. We didn't pick up any important SS, Gestapo or SD (Security Service). Then we went into Ostend, where we took up Port Security work with 273 Section. We remained there about four weeks.

Our job was to see what ships came in and to be on our guard in case anybody tried to sabotage us: any Germans, fifth columnists or spies who could have sneaked in via any neutral boats landing there.

We went out at about eight in the morning and came back at night. Each sergeant had to submit a report on the work he'd done each day. These duties were not rigidly defined, and we had more power than some of the officers when it came to breaches of security. Special privileges were bestowed on us in our work, and the ruling was that every assistance should be given to us in the execution of our authority.

On one particular day I was first back. Our officer, Captain Wilkins, said: 'Norman, I have got some bad news for you. I have to replace one of our sergeants in the front-line section who has been shot in the leg. As I have three German-speaking sergeants, I decided that whoever came back first would replace him.'

Fate, again, seemed to have played a hand, because why did I come back first that day? I was usually one of the last.

So I joined the Eighth Corps 53 Field Security section.

Brussels was interesting. I drove a captured field marshal (Field Marshal von Rundstedt) in a jeep through the city to be detained. He said to me: 'People are cheering today. When I was here, they never cheered us.'

'Yes,' I said. 'But you came as oppressors, not as liberators.' That was my first meeting with a high-ranking German officer.

From there, we went on to the south of Holland where we helped to liberate Eindhoven. The Philips factory was booby-trapped and some of our lads made it safe. Then, in October 1944, we went to Mill in the north of Holland, near Eindhoven, where we became static.

In the meantime, a very severe winter set in, and we stayed in Mill until the spring of 1945, when the advance took place again. We crossed the Rhine at Venlo into Germany, and picked up a few minor SS. We also arrested one mayor in charge of the local Gestapo and took him to prison. We were entering small villages and towns; then one day, when we were outside Celle, we received information that there was a concentration camp in the vicinity which the Germans wanted to hand over to us because the line of defence was very near at the time. The Wehrmacht major, under the truce of a white flag, came and spoke to one of the forward infantry section, who called us in and said that this camp, which was mainly a women's camp,* had very bad infectious diseases such as typhus, dysentery and cholera. They wanted us to take over the camp because they were afraid that if they left and the people there escaped, they would spread disease all over Germany.

After we had liberated Belsen camp, I made numerous arrests of some of the most notorious Nazis.

I arrested Field Marshal Fritz Erich von Manstein in one of the villages outside Plön. We'd been tipped off that he was there. He had been sacked by Hitler six months before the war ended. We also arrested Field Marshal Walther von Brauchitsch the same day. Both men had been demoted by Hitler for their failure in the Russian campaign.

I have clearer memories of von Manstein, because of the way he reacted when I told him he was under arrest. I ordered him to take off his shoelaces and braces, which is normal procedure

---

* Belsen camp originated in 1943. Before that, it was used as a Russian POW camp. The Germans killed 60,000 Russians there before they turned it into a concentration camp.

in these cases. He said to me: 'Do you realise that I am a field marshal? I expect to be arrested by someone from the same rank.'

I turned to him and said: 'Well, Field Marshal Montgomery is too busy and he asked me to do it!' There was no answer to that.

The most interesting arrest I made was that of Josef Keindel, who posed as a concentration camp inmate, a 'displaced person'. All inmates were entitled to extra rations, and anyone who asked for special ration cards had to be interviewed by me or one of my colleagues, to establish their identity.

When I saw him I instinctively felt there was something wrong about him. He didn't look to me as if he had suffered very much during the war. I bluffed him, during my interrogation, into admitting that he was the Commandant of Oranienburg camp. We had books full of names of some of the top Nazis, including Goebbels, Goering and Hitler, and I kept on looking through them but didn't find Keindel's name in my 'black book'.

Then, on the spur of the moment I said to him: 'You are not a concentration camp inmate. I know who you are.' He turned white and said: 'Well, I might as well tell you ... I was the Commandant of Oranienburg camp.'

My hunch had been correct, and I was so surprised at this that both of us were silent for quite a few minutes. Then Keindel said: 'Look – I'm willing to tell you where some of the people are hiding, and I can also tell you about some of the crimes that have been committed, as long as you don't hand me over to the Russians.'

I promised him not to do that. Instead, I handed all our prisoners over to the British Military Police to be detained, and I passed on all the information he gave me to the British Army HQ at Plön. Whether or not he was subsequently turned over to the Russians I don't know, but it made me feel good to have caught him. Kramer had been there, at Belsen, waiting for me to arrest him, and all I had to do was write out an arrest warrant. Keindel, however, was a different proposition altogether, and might have got away with it had he managed to get the relevant papers.

A few days later I went into a POW camp at Gromitz on the Baltic, where there were about 30,000 inmates, and I asked to see a man whom I'd been informed (by Keindel) was one of the top Gestapo in Lithuania. I went on my own to this camp, and when I told the German soldiers there that I wanted to see Mr X, they took me to his barrack. When I approached him I said: 'Are you Mr X?'

'Yes,' he said.

'You'll have to come with me,' I said. 'I must detain you. You are not a German soldier: you are a Gestapo agent.'

I then drove him from this camp up to Neustadt, where I handed him over to the Military Police with my arrest report. When I told Captain Stephen what I'd done, I got reprimanded for going on my own to arrest a notorious Gestapo man. I hadn't thought for a moment of the possible risks involved – of being shot or beaten up. He was perfectly right: I should never have gone by myself, but I took a chance and luckily nothing untoward happened.

I had heard a great deal about the terrible crimes of the Gestapo – how brutal they'd been to ordinary, innocent people – so that I felt pleased that I had the opportunity to arrest him.

Meanwhile, after I had had to leave Belsen at the beginning of May, no communication between Gena and me was possible at all – no post, no telephone, nothing – because the war was drawing to a close and life was chaotic. The war ended on 8 May. Gena and I both wrote letters to each other but never received them. I still thought about her all the time.

Early in July 1945, my mother had a very bad heart attack, so Keith Stephen gave me compassionate leave to go home and see her. I was flown from Hamburg to Bury St Edmunds. I was away for about ten days at the end of July, and on the day before I was due to return from England, Gena came up to my unit in Nieder

Klewitz, a village near the Baltic about four miles from Plön, with the Rabbi Hardman to try and find me, because she hadn't heard from me for months and didn't know where I was or even whether I was still alive.

When she arrived, Keith Stephen told her that I had gone on leave to London because my mother was ill, but that immediately I returned he would make sure that I visited her.

As soon as I got back to Germany and before I even had a chance to unpack, Keith Stephen insisted that I go to Belsen immediately. He said to me: 'Norman, go down to Belsen where your fiancée is waiting for you. She is extremely worried as she hasn't heard anything from you. Make arrangements for your wedding and then come back.'

I had to drive from Nieder Klewitz to Belsen, which is a journey of about 350 kilometres. I set off straight away, at about 10 a.m. and arrived in Belsen about 2 p.m.

I arrived to find that the old camp had been burned down by the flame-throwers, to minimise the risk of further disease spreading. The ex-inmates (alias 'displaced persons') were now living in the old brick barracks which used to be occupied by the Wehrmacht. When I found out where they were, I saw Gena's mother, who was very happy to see me. Gena was out but due back any minute.

Her mother said: 'You hide here, behind the curtain, and I'll call her when she returns.'

Gena was taken aback when I suddenly appeared – and a bit upset because of my absence, but when I explained to her the reason I had gone home to England she understood.

She asked me how I felt about her now. I said I felt just the same as before, and I told her I'd arranged for us to get married on 7 October. That was in about six weeks' time.

'Are you sure *I* want to marry *you?*' she asked me. I said: 'Well, I've made all the arrangements, and it's taken me a long time.' British servicemen had to have permission from the Army to marry foreign nationals.

I asked her how she felt about me. She said: 'Well, I don't really know you. All I know is that I've been missing you.'

I had to get back to my unit to complete my work. I suggested that Gena come up there a few days before our wedding and I would find her a place to stay with some German people near where I was stationed.

Gena arrived around 1 October and stayed in a farmhouse near our unit. It was the first opportunity we'd had since we met to spend some days together and really get to know each other. We had so much in common that in our conversations it seemed to me that I'd known her for years and years.

My very good friend and fellow sergeant, 'Lulu' McKitrick, made all the arrangements for our wedding. He was a wonderful friend with a heart of gold. He managed to get hold of a British silk parachute and we found a German dressmaker from Nieder Klewitz who created a wedding dress out of it for Gena – in three days.

We were married in a synagogue at Lübeck at 3 p.m. – a coincidence, as the time that Gena and Belsen were liberated was also 3 o'clock, so this, as I saw it, was another piece in the puzzle or pattern of our romance.

She looked radiant, though a little pale, which was probably due to worry about her mother's state of health. Mrs Goldfinger was recovering from typhus and still too ill to travel to Lübeck for our wedding.

'Lulu' organised a beautiful bouquet of roses for Gena, and a wedding feast at our unit's headquarters. All the higher officers attended, and also among our guests was Archie Mansfield, a fellow sergeant who is now in his eighties. He was stationed in Neustadt and I was quite friendly with him. After he read the newspaper reports of our attendance at the fortieth anniversary commemoration day at Belsen in 1985, he phoned me and I invited him to our ruby wedding celebrations. He still remembered all the details of our wedding day.

Our honeymoon was brief. A few days after we married I had

to move on to Neustadt and I rented a room for us with a German teacher's family called Müller. We were only there for a couple more days, as we received notification that Gena must go to England. At that time a military ruling specified that no British subject or non-German was allowed to live in Germany. This applied to Gena, who had become a British subject by marriage, and I was granted compassionate leave to take her to England.

Kramer was eventually hanged. He went into a Wehrmacht compound, where the German soldiers beat him up. It took about six weeks for him to be patched up and put on trial. He was tried at Lüneburg with the other SS from Belsen. About 75 per cent of them were hanged, including Kramer, Dr Klein and most of the women guards. Others received sentences of between ten years and life imprisonment.

9

Breathing with my Freedom

While the British Army was fast approaching on that Sunday in April 1945, life was going on much as normal for us in Belsen: processions of transports in and out of the camp, more shootings, more bloodshed. It never crossed our minds that freedom was just around the corner, and we had no advance warning of what was about to happen. It seemed as if the war would last forever.

I was in the hospital surgery sterilising my instruments, taking them out of the tank and sorting them, when I heard behind me the voice of Frau Kramer, the wife of the camp commandant. She and Dr Klein were talking together. I opened my ears wider and I heard Frau Kramer say: 'My husband went to meet them, so they should be here very soon.' She didn't mention who *they* were, and I wondered to whom she was referring. I thought: 'There must be something going on.' My heart was beating hard, and I had butterflies in my stomach.

Then they went into the adjoining waiting room. I saw Frau Kramer standing at the window that looked on to the outskirts of the camp. With her was a German woman *kapo*, with short blond hair and wearing tight trousers, a prisoner who had been selected by the Nazis as a guard.

I went in there and stood behind them, looking out of the window. I could see tanks, marked with a white star, passing by on the main road outside. The woman *kapo* put her hands on her hips and said she never believed that the foreign Allies would enter German soil. She wanted to play up to Kramer's wife, to impress her and show that she was on her side.

Because the Nazis were standing by fully armed, I couldn't express any emotion at this scene outside. I couldn't show my feelings of joy that somebody had come to release us. I was still scared. They could do anything with us. I just had to carry on with my work and not say a word.

When the gates opened and the tanks entered the camp, we heard voices speaking in all languages through the loudspeakers: English, Polish, German. 'We have come to liberate you. You are all free. The Nazis have got nothing to say to you.' It was the happiest moment of my life, and one of the most fantastic experiences that could happen to anyone.

The British troops came to the door of the hospital and we gave them some water to wash their hands. The Nazis were still there, with pistols in their holsters, and we were still afraid. It was a strange combination and we couldn't understand it: here, on one side, the British; there, on the other side, armed Nazi guards.

The Nazis were walking around like this for two days, until they were ordered to assemble outside the *Kommandantur* (British headquarters) by the main gate and to lay down their arms. When they were arrested I wept tears of happiness.

They marched past, their faces expressionless and yet still retaining a cocky, arrogant stance. They had been so brainwashed by Hitler into believing that they would win the war that they must have felt a sense of unreality about being arrested.

Some of the inmates were half-dead and unable to grasp that they were finally free, while those who could move about were gasping for food or trying to make plans to find other members of their families. They had to wait several weeks until quarantine restrictions were lifted.

About 20 women inmates rushed screaming into the rooms of the SS women, grabbing clothes and any other items they could find. They wanted the satisfaction of breaking into those women's barracks, their homes. It was a way of cooling their blood after the horrors of the previous months.

I can remember walking from the hospital to the living quarters and seeing a British tank moving towards me. It was a beautiful sunny day and I was looking around for a flower or some grass to throw as a symbol of gratitude, but there was nothing except dust and sand.

When I got into work the day after we were liberated, I found a lot of ammunition lying around the hospital: pistols and rifles, dumped there as if some of the SS had left in a hurry. There were piles of Nazi uniforms, too, so the guards must have changed into civilian clothes before making their getaway. One of them must have been the hospital dentist, whom I had seen in his uniform and still armed with a pistol talking to a British soldier the previous day. Maria, the Polish nurse, had obtained some civilian clothes for him and helped him to escape.

Some of them fled into the woods behind the camp. Others mingled among our people inside the camp. They were trying to pass as inmates by wandering around in shabby clothes, but they looked very furtive.

It is difficult to describe the meaning of freedom: to be able to walk where you want to walk, do what you want to do, say what you want to say . . . it is a wonderful, wonderful feeling.

On the second day of liberation, two British Army sergeants came into the hospital to look for weapons and some SS men whom they suspected were hiding somewhere in the hospital barrack. I was in another room at the time, and Maria called me to tell me they were waiting there.

I returned to the front of the hospital and saw the two sergeants standing in the waiting room. I said to one of them: 'Do you speak German?'

'Why?' he asked me.

I said: 'I just thought you would. I have a feeling that you understand German.'

I was right, and we conversed together. I think he liked my way of speaking. He asked me what I was doing there and I told him I'd been working as a nurse.

I liked him and was impressed when he told me about his work trying to track down the Nazis and to see justice done.

The following day he brought Helen Kulka, a German anti-Nazi secretary, with him and she took down everything I said about what had happened while I was in the camp, how many people died each night, where some of the Nazis were hiding, and also details about Plaszov and Auschwitz camps.

Apart from the one day when he was ill, he kept coming in every day and made a point of seeing me. I told him I knew only two English phrases: 'The sky is blue' and 'The sun is shining', the two expressions which I'd remembered from my childhood in Poland. I grew fond of him, and he grew fond of me.

One day he said he would like me to come to the Officers' Mess for dinner. I said I would have to ask my mother. She wasn't keen on the idea because she thought he may have been a married man, or that he could be like a lot of sailors with a sweetheart in each port. She said: 'Be careful. Maybe you had better take a friend with you.' So I took Tola with me, and we went for dinner in the Officers' Mess.

Because of the typhus epidemic, Norman had to ask special permission for us to leave the camp. We had to be disinfected.

The tables were laid with crisp white tablecloths and wonderfully decorated with flowers – a sight I hadn't seen for many years. I said to Norman: 'What is all this? Are you expecting special guests?'

He said: 'You are the special guest. This is our engagement party.' And yet he never actually proposed to me! He took it for granted that I would accept.

Then Captain Stephen, his commanding officer, and other colleagues came over and congratulated me. I said to myself: 'They must have had too much to drink.' I didn't take it seriously because, really and truly, my mind wasn't on getting married or on any romantic ties. I just wanted to breathe with my freedom, with the fresh air. I wanted to leave that environment and not have that smell of decay all around me. I was in a trance, a daze.

But Norman tried to pin me to a decision. After dinner he took us back to the barracks. The following day he came over and wanted to give me a kiss. I pushed him away, because in those days a kiss was something very special. He said: 'You are my fiancée.'

I said: 'You don't know me, and I don't know you. We are strangers.'

He took off a ring he was wearing and put it on my finger. Then he typed a few lines, in English, on a sheet of paper which explained that I was engaged to a British sergeant, that help would be provided for me in his absence and that I should wait for his return to get married. I was the happiest woman in the world.

The following day he had to leave Belsen. The war was still on and his unit was moving on to Plön.

A few days after we were liberated, the British Army were needed elsewhere and we were left in the temporary charge of Hungarian troops, but this proved to be an unsatisfactory arrangement. They were playing around with their guns and shooting people at random. They killed several inmates. I don't know if they were drunk, or maybe they wanted to test their authority. We were terrified, and we appealed to the British to return their troops at once.

After Norman left for Plön I was very busy, nursing and counselling large numbers of people coming in from other camps. They stayed and registered in Belsen and came looking for relatives. After several weeks the gates of the camp were opened and people were free to come and go, although most were still too weak to venture far. Many inmates continued to die, from the food (the effects of eating a normal diet after prolonged malnutrition) and the sustained shock of their imprisonment.

There was a great deal of work to do. People were so helpless.

I stayed and did what I could. I talked to them and tried to calm them down. I was unable to leave the camp as my mother was seriously ill with typhus. Before he left, Norman had given me permission to take her into the hospital. I was sleeping in the ward next to her, so as to be on call in case she needed me.

The moment she stepped into the hospital bed, her temperature went sky-high. She was like fire, she was absolutely burning, and I was sponging and washing her to keep the heat down. I was frightened she would get pneumonia, so I used to turn her from one side to the other. It was quite a job. She was very ill indeed, but with my common sense and the little knowledge I had I brought her back to life.

I had a small cupboard where I kept a few medicines. I gave her suppositories and injected her twice a day with sympatol to strengthen her heart, so that I would not have any guilty feelings about not doing all that was in my power to do.

I tied her with towels around the waist to the bottom of the bed, to keep her upright, and spoonfed her with liquids.

At first there were no doctors around to ask: 'Am I doing the right thing?' but I could see that after a few days she was responding.

Soon, doctors started coming in – French, Belgian, British. I remember in particular one French doctor, who was slim and wore glasses. I called him over to examine my mother. We spoke in German.

He said: 'Are you a doctor?'

I said: 'No, but I hope to be one day.'

He clapped me on the shoulder and said: 'You've done a wonderful job. Remarkable! She is on the mend.'

I watched her all the time and kept on hoping. Today, I would have been reluctant to experiment with medicines and injections, but at that time, seeing the way my mother was lying there almost unconscious and in such agony, I thought: 'I have got to try.'

She felt indebted to me, and told everybody afterwards that I had saved her life. I was proud of that, really proud.

During the same period, a Polish boy was brought in on a stretcher. He had a terrible boil on his head. He remembered me as a little girl. 'I know you,' he said. 'Your family brought shoes to my father.' His father had been a shoe repairer in Poland. Their name was Bukowsky. They were a Catholic family.

He said: 'I don't want anyone to touch me, only you. I don't trust anybody else.'

'I'm not a doctor,' I said.

'I don't care,' he replied. 'Whatever you do with me, it will be all right.'

He was terrified and begged me to operate on this huge boil, which was almost as big as his head. 'I'll do what I can,' I told him. I had no other choice but to tell the other girls who were working with me: 'Sterilise the instruments.'

I put on a mask, gave the boy some morphine, cut the boil in half and then around it, and applied some dressing.

Thank goodness he survived. I had taken a great chance. After a few days he was taken to Sweden for a period of convalescence.

It gave me so much confidence, the way he said: 'Nobody else but you.' I felt like a grown-up, qualified surgeon. It was a wonderful feeling to help somebody, though I was terribly scared to perform an operation without any basic knowledge. I didn't act like a twenty-one-year-old. In many ways, and through the experiences I'd had, I acted more like someone twice my age. Such experiences educate you as to what life is really about.

I managed to see a doctor about the bites on my leg, which had turned septic despite my efforts with salted water. When he saw the state of my leg, he was horrified and told me it could easily have turned gangrenous. He gave me some yellow cream and slowly things got better.

The British Army did much to boost our morale. From the private soldier to senior officer level, they tried to help us in whatever way they could. They organised transports from England of meat, chocolates, Players cigarettes. In April I remember

Norman bringing us crisp round loaves, the first white bread we had seen for years, and two oranges for my mother.

The troops dug up food supplies which had been buried by the Nazis outside the camp, and distributed them among the inmates. They found tins of meat, jams, fruit and other preserves. The Nazis wanted to pretend to the liberating forces that there was no food left in the camp and that the SS, too, had been starving.

Many other goods came to light in this way. The Dutch soldiers discovered cases of champagne and other alcoholic drinks in the cellar of Kramer's quarters, and these were shared among all the inmates. Cases of watches, stolen from the inmates, were also found beneath the soil in Kramer's garden and distributed – one case to every barrack. Each of us was allowed to choose a watch. Many years later I gave mine to Norman as a present.

People from the surrounding farms would come into the camp and barter, keen to do business with us. Through the hospital window I exchanged my mother's watch for a chicken. I cut it up and every day I boiled a piece and gave her the soup. A chicken was like caviare, a luxury item. Other meats had already been flown in by the Red Cross but were too heavy for most inmates to digest. I could only eat small helpings and very slowly, because my stomach had shrunk so much. It would take months, maybe even years, to readjust to a normal diet. In fact, I am still doing this today.

Some people were so hungry that they were stuffing themselves with almost any food they could find, which wasn't good for them.

After the quarantine restrictions were lifted, some people travelled through Germany and Poland from camp to camp looking for relatives, but I had to stay in Belsen as my mother was still very ill and I couldn't leave her on her own.

During the spring and summer months of 1945, the Red Cross and St John's Ambulance Brigade did wonderful work, bringing in supplies of clothes and food, and generally assisting with the running of the camp.

As a way of lifting our spirits, Lady Montgomery (the Field Marshal's wife) of the Red Cross organised some concerts in a big marquee in which the inmates participated. In the first concert I sang two songs in German. The dress I was wearing was one that I'd made – with a little help from another girl – out of long drapes of white surgical gauze.

They tried to bring out people's individual talents. There were some very gifted artists, including a Polish woman called Eva, who dressed up in a Tyrolean costume and took the main part in a play as well as directing it, and a pianist, who accompanied me and other singers.

The highlight of the entertainment was the evening when Yehudi Menuhin came and performed for us. We hadn't heard music of such quality for many years. It was wonderful that such a talented man should give up his time to appear before us. We were very touched that he came to Belsen. It was a wonderful human gesture. He was a charming, good-looking man. I met him again in Israel in 1984.

Lady Montgomery was a happy, pleasant woman with a round face and red cheeks. She took me to the Officers' Mess where we had a dance together. She taught me the Hokey-Cokey!

Meanwhile, I had lost all trace of Norman. Three months went by and I heard nothing. I'd written several letters, but received no word of his whereabouts.

We hadn't seen each other more than half a dozen times, because he had been so busy rounding up the SS. It was secretive work; he couldn't talk about what it involved, and I didn't ask him.

During this time, about five weeks after the Liberation, Major Burney came on the scene. His job was to oversee the camp on behalf of the Allies, and he was put in charge of the inventory: food, medical supplies and so on. He had two Czech girl translators working for him, and we became friendly. We lived on the same floor in the brick barracks previously occupied by the

German soldiers. All the inmates had moved there from the old wooden barracks which had been burned down by the flame-throwers.

Life became more civilised. We had proper bedrooms with clean bunks, water and sanitation. We felt like human beings again. My mother and I shared a room with Tola and another Polish girl, Irka. Irka had been our *blockowa* at Belsen. She had also worked as a *blockowa* at Auschwitz, although I didn't know her when I was there. I think she must have carried some guilt with her, because it seemed as if she was trying to be nice to us, especially to my mother – as if she wanted to make amends in some way. We had no idea what she'd been up to before, and we didn't really care; we were too thrilled to be free.

Anyway, she didn't stay long. She met a Polish (non-Jewish) man called Michael, who had also been in Auschwitz, and they soon went off together to live in South America.

I slept badly, because in my mind I continued to hear shots and shouts in the night. The Nazis' voices were always in our ears, always with us, haunting us.

The two girl translators invited me in for coffee one day. Major Burney came and asked questions about me: whether I was in love with Norman, and so on. He couldn't speak a word of German and the girls translated on my behalf. They had told him that I'd met a British sergeant but had heard nothing from him for about three months. He took an interest and wrote away to Norman's headquarters on my behalf.

At that time other people had been arriving from England – including Rabbi Leslie Hardman, the British Army chaplain, who arrived three or four days after liberation. My mother told him that I was engaged to this man and had no idea where he was. He said he would go to England and make enquiries about his background and credentials: whether or not he was already married.

He came back and told Major Burney: 'He's all right – he's

not married, and the family is nice.' So he said to me: 'If you like, I will take you to visit him where he is stationed.'

We travelled 300 kilometres to Plön, where his unit was based, but he wasn't there. Captain Stephen, Norman's commanding officer, told us he had had to go to England. To me, a word is a bond, and I lost some of my faith in him. I returned to Belsen and decided that I would have to forget about him.

Two days went by. I was outside in the garden when my mother called from our room upstairs: 'Gena, come up, please.' I went up into the room and didn't see anybody else at first. Then Norman, who was hiding behind the curtain, came out and tried to kiss me, but I pushed him away. I said: 'I don't think we should carry on.'

He explained that he had come over especially to settle the date of our wedding. He kept apologising, and told me that his mother had been taken ill and that he'd had to go home to England to visit her.

I still wasn't sure. I felt hurt that he'd broken his promise to me, but he begged me to forgive him. I thought of how much I liked him, and particularly of the work he had done in bringing people to justice, and I said: 'All right, I'll marry you.'

In the meantime, Lady Abrahams, a councillor in Finchley, who had come to Belsen with the Red Cross, asked me to go and see her. She was protective towards me. She called me into her office one day and took me to one side, pointing out the big step I was about to take in life. She asked: 'Are you sure you know what you are doing?'

'Yes,' I said. 'I do realise what I am taking on – and I'm looking forward to it.'

On the day of our marriage, 7 October 1945, a telegram arrived from Dr Thorek, my mother's cousin in Chicago, who had heard that we were alive and in Belsen. My mother was not yet well enough to come to the wedding and told me later that a fellow had run from barrack to barrack shouting: 'Mrs Goldfinger! There's a telegram from Chicago.' It was nice of him to show such an interest in us and we rang him after we got to England.

It had been my original hope that Dr Thorek would introduce me to medical school in America. I have no regrets now, but if I had my time over again I should love to have qualified as a doctor.

We were married in Lübeck, at a synagogue which the Germans had used as a stable during the war. Ours was the first post-war wedding to take place there.

Rabbi Leslie Hardman married us, and I was given away by Captain Stephen, a charming man.

About thirty people came, mostly non-Jewish. Apart from myself, there were only three other women present. All the men wore their Army caps as a mark of respect. Instead of the traditional white satin-fringed canopy with embroidered lettering used at Jewish weddings, we had to improvise with a piece of cloth draped on four poles.

After the ceremony, we had a reception at Army HQ in Plön. The meal was chicken stew followed by some dessert, but I was too full of emotion to eat much. I was only just beginning to realise what a personal landmark I was facing in my life. I felt sad, too, that because the journey would have been too strenuous for her my mother could not be present.

At the time I was very shy, spoke little English and got swept along by everything. In some ways I would have liked a little longer to think about it, but Norman was so determined to marry me that I just gave in, and I'm happy now that I did. I really believe we were meant for each other.

We spent our honeymoon night and a few more days in Nieder Klewitz, where he had been given a room.

Then Norman had to move on to Neustadt. Shortly afterwards, he had permission to travel with me to England. Now that I had become a British citizen by marriage, I had to leave Germany.

We travelled in an Army car, stopping in Brussels, where we spent the night in a hotel. In the morning we boarded an Army ship. I was the only civilian. The other passengers were all ATS girls and soldiers. The crossing was absolutely terrible, and I shall never forget it. Everyone was vomiting. But at least I felt in safe hands. There might have been mines in the sea, but I was not afraid any more. Nothing could remotely compare with what I had lived through over the past six years.

I felt very lonely, especially knowing that I was going to a strange country and having had to leave my mother behind in Germany. I cried all the way. I felt guilty about leaving her, but the moment I arrived in England I started to set the wheels in motion to bring her across.

On 10 November 1945, we arrived at Tilbury. All of Fleet Street had heard we were coming, and dozens of reporters and photographers were waiting for us at St Pancras Station. They wanted 'A Story, A Story . . .' The papers were full of banner headlines: 'The Bride from Belsen is here!' I felt as if I had come from outer space.

All I wanted was to hide away. I was embarrassed at the star treatment – and so tired. I'd had so little sleep for so long that I often used to say: 'After the war is over I would like to sleep for three months.'

10

I Touched the Bricks . . .

After I arrived in England I was so full with my new life, with the feeling that I could at last open a window and let in fresh air, the feeling that I had come out of the darkness.

We started married life in my in-laws' first-floor flat in Hendon, North London. We had one of their five bedrooms: a little room with a bed, wardrobe, dressing table – and a small radio, given to Norman by Philips Engineering in Germany as a token of their gratitude after he had helped to dismantle a bomb in one of the company's factories.

The day after our arrival, more reporters called, hoping for a story. They plied me with questions about my life in the camps. It was very hard for me to talk about it because I was thrilled just to be alive and those experiences were still fresh and painful. I also spoke little English.

I had also – reluctantly – to leave my mother behind. Whereas my marriage to Norman had automatically made me a British citizen, Mother was still regarded as a foreigner and my father-in-law had to apply for permission to bring her over to England. We kept in touch by letter.

Some Polish friends of mine were living in the same block as we were at Belsen after the Liberation, and they looked after Mother. They were very kind to her. They were political prisoners – two brothers and a sister: Bolek, Edward and Stefa. The Nazis had caught them listening to an overseas news broadcast and sent them first to Auschwitz, where their own mother had died, and then to Belsen. They live in Warsaw today and I am still in touch with them.

I was so thin and undernourished that for about two years I had to have extra rations to build me up: bananas, oranges, butter, cheese, meat. My stomach was in bad shape and I had to be extremely careful about my diet.

My general health was poor, especially my lungs, and I had to attend the Middlesex Hospital as an outpatient every six weeks for an examination. An X-ray showed a scar on one lung, but the additional nourishment helped heal some of the worst damage.

My back was painful because of the pressure on my spine from all that standing, particularly in the square at Plaszov. I went to see an orthopaedic specialist and for many years I had to wear a surgical corset every day. Now and again I still have to put it on.

I am a terrible patient and I don't like to be ill. I am still very strict about what I eat and drink. Alcohol upsets me, and I stick to plain meals so as not to have any regrets afterwards. I can't always eat all the dishes that I cook for my family and for guests. If we are invited out to dinner, I hold a glass of wine and sip from it, just to be sociable.

I used to get very tired during the day and I suffered from depression for some time because, although I was happy to be in England, it was difficult to push away the memories of my sisters and brothers who had died, and all the experiences I had gone through. I never liked to show that I was depressed. I used to go into my room and cry. After a good cry one feels lighter inside and more able to cope. I smiled on the surface, but the deep sadness was always with me and always will be.

Norman was still in the Army, and two weeks after he brought me over he had to go back to Germany. We corresponded in German. About six weeks later I was amazed to find that I was pregnant. I wasn't very happy about this and wondered how it was possible after so many years of malnutrition and menstrual difficulties. I felt I needed more time to adjust to my new way of life before being ready to face the challenge of motherhood. I was frightened and, emotionally, very unprepared. I even considered having an abortion, but in those days abortion was illegal and, in any case, it was against my religious beliefs.

I wrote to Norman and told him the news, and he was delighted. My doctor said: 'Cheer up. Be happy.' But I had a very bad pregnancy. I was terribly sick and couldn't keep any food down. I lived on boiled potatoes and warm milk.

Towards the end of my pregnancy Norman was demobbed. He returned to England in July 1946 and went straight into his father's fur trading business. Norman's father and his father's brother were both partners, and his sister Rose worked with them as a secretary. His father and uncle didn't get on too well. The uncle was a difficult man, a bit of a slave driver, who always wanted to have the upper hand and never appreciated Norman's honest hard work. His father was quieter and more gentle. After he passed away, Norman was supposed to take over his father's shares, but we discovered that his uncle had kept the majority of them. Eventually, Norman bought out his uncle's share in the business, and that eased the situation. His uncle left the business, and a couple of years later he died. Our son, Harris, and our daughters, Hilary and Bernice, now help him.

My parents-in-law were very kind to me, especially Norman's father, whom I came to regard as my own father. He used to come into the bedroom every morning and bring me a cup of tea, a biscuit and an apple, and maybe some toast. I felt very sick and had little appetite, but he said: 'You must eat,' and he was most helpful. My mother-in-law was getting over a heart attack and had to take things easy.

My three sisters-in-law, all unmarried, also lived in the flat. They used to stare at me a lot. I felt a bit strange at first because I didn't know their ways or the correct way to behave in England. I helped in the house, cleaning the floors and doing some cooking. Although my knowledge of English was limited, I sensed that they were talking about me. I kept hearing the word 'she', and I asked my father-in-law: 'What does it mean – *she*?' I think they felt that they were one-up on me, that I was some kind of inferior being because I had come from a concentration camp. I tried to ignore it.

From the moment I arrived I was determined to learn English. I felt so fortunate to be able to come to England and start a new, free life, a life without fear.

There were no colleges open immediately after the war, but I had a little private tuition, and after a couple of months I was able to speak and understand the language to a certain extent. I read the papers and listened a lot to the radio.

When I first came to England, people seemed very preoccupied with themselves. Some said: 'We also had a hard time. We were bombed and had to live in shelters. We had to sleep in the Underground.'

I said: 'Yes, I'm sure it must have been bad, but at least you weren't living in constant fear that someone would hit you or shoot you at any moment, or that you might starve.' These people lived in a different world. They had blackouts, but they had amusements, dances . . . They were able to go out and enjoy themselves.

However, I had no wish to get drawn into discussions or comparisons of that kind. Some people are thick-skinned and don't let any bad or unpleasant experiences affect them. I took no notice and carried on trying to make the best of my new life.

In the meantime, when I was several months pregnant, my mother's immigration papers came through. I bought a bunch of red roses and went to Victoria Station to meet her. I waited there for hours and hours, but there was no sign of her, and when I eventually returned to the flat she was already there. Somehow we had missed each other.

Mother had travelled to England with a Polish girl and boy who were both inmates at Belsen, and heading for Manchester. They looked after her throughout the journey. Their relations, too, had applied for visas for them to enter Britain. When I spoke to her later, the girl told me that her arm was aching because

Mother had been clutching her, terrified, throughout the journey.

The reunion was wonderful. Seeing her again was the joy of my life. She was wearing a navy suit with a white blouse, and she had a new hairdo. She had put on weight and looked much healthier.

She was happy to see me, too, and I noticed her looking at me for a long time. I told her I was pregnant and she said: 'You're *not?*' She could hardly believe it!

She moved into another flat on the same floor which belonged to a woman who was selling up to live abroad. I joined her there after the baby arrived.

I was in labour for nearly two days, and in agony. Hilary weighed 7¼ pounds when she was born. The midwife at Edgware General Hospital took the baby in her arms and gazed at her for several minutes. She said: 'I've delivered hundreds of babies but never seen such a beautiful one as this.' I was thrilled.

When I came home from hospital, Millie, a friend of Norman's mother, was waiting at the top of the stairs. She took Hilary from me and made a fuss of her.

Afterwards, I lost a lot of weight. I became skinny as a stick. My doctor told me I must gain a few pounds. The local greengrocer – Welsh's in Hendon – gave me some oranges. They used to go to the back of the shop and pick out the best Bramley's cooking apples for me.

One day after Hilary was born Norman and I went to the cinema. I had a green ration book, the type issued to mothers to buy sweets for their children. The assistant in the confectionery kiosk asked me: 'When were you pregnant?' She thought I must have adopted a child because I was so slim and I was wearing all my normal clothes.

I lived in a mixed neighbourhood and many people, Jewish and non-Jewish, knew about my background, as they had read about me in the newspapers and seen my picture there. Everybody was pleasant to me, and although it was hard to shake off the wariness that I'd acquired in the camps I found that many people I met –

strangers – seemed genuinely interested to hear my story. After Hilary was born, I used to take her to the local park in her pram. I met other mothers there with their babies, and we used to sit and talk, and they would ask me about my wartime experiences.

I used to take Hilary on my lap and rock her to sleep. She was a very poor sleeper and used to wake up several times in the night. My own sleep pattern was erratic, and I used to dream a lot about the camps. Many times Norman had to wake me because I was having a nightmare, screaming in my sleep. I still suffer from nightmares, though less often now. I just have to live with it.

Even now, when I watch a film about the Second World War, I have to pinch myself and ask: 'Am I really here? Could I ever have gone through all that?'

When we were first married I didn't mind going without, or wearing the same dress all the time, and I would wash the same tablecloth every day and keep using it because I treasured every object, however small, in my possession.

I didn't mind doing household chores like washing shirts, ironing or cooking, though I knew little about cooking until my mother came over to England and taught me.

I appreciated simple things – like listening to the birds singing in the early mornings . . . a bowl of fruit on the dining-room table . . . a piece of material which I bought for five shillings and from which, helped by my mother, I made myself a dress. These meant more to me than thousands of pounds.

When Norman and I moved with Mother into our house in Edgware in 1954, I touched the bricks on the wall outside. I stroked those bricks and said: 'That's our house. We've worked for it.' It was a feeling of achievement and satisfaction after all the years of deprivation.

Mother developed agoraphobia immediately after the war. This was understandable, because of the shock of those experiences which stayed with her and the fear she had that there might be

Nazis prowling around the streets of North London. This made her afraid to leave the house.

She sometimes ventured out of the front door, holding on to me and taking a few steps to the right or left, and that was enough for her. She used to sit in an armchair in the living room by the window. Everybody in the neighbourhood knew her and used to wave to her as they passed the house.

When Hilary and Bernice were small, she used to sit with them in a little yard at the back of our flats in Hendon. I put the pram under a tree there. She loved being with my children, and they all adored her. After each one was born and came home from the hospital, she felt she had to be the one to wash the first nappy. She grabbed it and rushed into the bathroom to wash it. She said: 'That brings luck!'

With Harris, my third child, she and Norman had a fight over who should be allowed to perform this ritual. He was just as keen to do it!

In all the twenty-seven years she lived with us, until she died in 1973, I could never leave her alone because she would feel afraid and insecure. I always had to have somebody at home, even if I only went down the road to the shops. Millie, who was with us for twenty years, would come and babysit for Mother as well as for my children. Sometimes I had to call on my next-door neighbour. When the children were older, they took turns in looking after her. They used to call her 'Babi', a Jewish term of endearment for 'grandmother'.

The furthest she travelled was to Harris's Barmitzvah at Wembley Town Hall, a few miles away, on 9 July 1966. Our doctor came and took her there in his car. She only stayed for a little while and then wanted to come home.

At Yom Kippur she used to sit in her chair by the window and pray the whole day. From six o'clock in the evening until 7.30 the following evening, she would not say a word to anybody. Her belief, which she had learned from her parents, was that during the year one says so many things which are unnecessary or perhaps trivial, that reserving one day a year for silence is a way of purifying one's mind.

At first, my children couldn't understand this. 'Why doesn't she speak?' they said. I told them not to disturb her because she was praying, and when the fast was over they asked her why she had remained silent. They wanted to know direct from her, and so she told them, and afterwards they left her alone.

In her later years Mother developed such a fear of going hungry that she would go upstairs to bed with a flask of hot milk, a cup or glass, and some bread rolls. She used to tuck the rolls underneath her arm and say: 'I don't want a plate. I'll take them like this.' That must have been a throwback to the camps.

Sometimes our grandson, Adam, only a toddler at the time, would carry her handbag containing various papers, some rolls, and her passport, which she treasured. She was so proud to be a British citizen – to feel that she really belonged here.

In the morning she would usually bring the flask and rolls downstairs again, but she would have finished drinking from the flask.

She slept badly. Many times in the night I would go into her room to see how she was. She suffered from serious stomach attacks and gallstones, but she was terrified of going to hospital and having an operation, so she had pills to relieve the pain and had to watch her diet carefully. She was prescribed Valium and sleeping tablets, too, at various times.

She used to have a little weep on the quiet, but basically, she was a happy person. Through her dignity and charm she managed to conceal any personal discomfort.

She learned to speak and read English well and soon switched completely from Polish to English newspapers. You could ask her almost anything about world affairs and she would be knowledge-able enough to have the right answers.

She used to love dancing. A waltz was her favourite. If she heard a waltz on the radio or television, she would jump up and grab Norman or myself and say 'Come on' and we'd have a little turn around the living room.

She loved opera, and for her birthday one year I bought her an Elisabeth Schwarzkopf album. We put this record on the radiogram really loud so that she could hear it upstairs on the day.

Each year we all stood outside her room and sang 'Happy Birthday to you', and I organised a party for her. She enjoyed that. Although she had suffered such a lot, she had a real sparkle about her, and I could always imagine her as a young person.

She was very good-looking and liked nice clothes. I remember her telling me that after my father died she had had plenty of opportunities to remarry. She had still been quite young and people wanted to introduce her to eligible men, but she said she wasn't interested because she didn't want her children to have a stepfather. We had never discussed this before. Our shared suffering in the ghetto and the camps had created a closer bond, enabling us to talk together more freely than ever before.

There were occasional moments which brought back memories of the camps – like a newspaper article, for instance. One of us would say: 'Remember this?'

Mother was always grateful to me for saving her life. To anyone who visited us, she would say that if she were to talk day and night for a year it would not be long enough to complete the tale of what happened to us during those years. And so she used to say: 'Better not to know about it.'

Between ourselves, we shared many tears as we talked, but we realised that it was futile to dwell on our experiences. We thought: 'We can't get those people back; we can't erase the pain we endured; the best years of our lives and our health can never be restored.'

Holidays or festivals were the kinds of family occasions that tended to trigger off her tears, times when she recalled having her nine children around her.

My house was always full when the children were young. They

often had their friends in, and I always seemed to be making mounds of sandwiches.

On Jewish festivals such as the Jewish New Year and Yom Kippur, I do a huge bake and put it all in the freezer weeks in advance. I bake lots of cakes – strudel and cheesecake – and we also have chopped liver, salad, avocados and various 'dips'.

When my mother was alive, the local rabbi used to come round at about one o'clock, after the Jewish New Year service at the synagogue. Because she was agoraphobic, she could never attend the synagogue and so the rabbi came to the house every year to blow the *shofar*, which is a kind of horn. Tradition has it that through the sound of the *shofar* his prayer goes up to God.

I have never been back to Poland. Neither my mother nor I wanted to return, having lost so many relations and friends there. We wanted to get right away and begin a new life.

Soon after we were liberated, I gave our old address in Cracow to a Polish woman friend of mine who was also looking for some relations. I thought there might be somebody in our family who was still alive there.

Who should she come across but Marcus? We hadn't seen or heard of one another since that night the Gestapo came to our flat and Willek locked Marcus in the corridor. He had been in a concentration camp in Germany and he was wondering whether Mother and I, or anyone else in the family, had survived. Many Polish people whom we used to know believed that our entire family must have perished.

Marcus now lives in London and we keep in touch. We lost trace of Soul, too, until he arrived in England long after the war. He had been in the Russian work camp. We were reunited here in London 19 years after the end of the war. He now lives in Israel and both his son and daughter are married. There is a great difference in our ages, and we see so little of each other that on the rare occasions when we do get together we talk about things that are happening now, in the present.

It is the same situation with my sister, Sala, who also lives in Israel. When Norman and I go there on business or for a holiday we usually see Sala and Soul, as well as visiting my mother's grave in Jerusalem. She lived tò be 99. In order to fulfil her last wish we had arranged for her burial in Jerusalem. Her dream had always been to visit the Western Wall to give thanks for her survival, but because of her agoraphobia she had been unable to make the journey while she was alive.

One day, when we were living in the flats at Hendon, the telephone rang and a woman's voice said in Polish: 'You'd better sit down while I tell you who I am.' When she told me, I really needed that chair! It was Karola, who had worked in the kitchen at Belsen. I never thought I would see her again. Her husband was taken to Mauthausen and hanged. She now lives in Belgium and was visiting her son Janek in England at the time. He was in hiding with a Polish family during the war, and they saved his life. He married a Belgian girl and Norman and I went to his wedding in Antwerp in 1959.

In the early years of our marriage, I started trying to put on paper my account of the things I had experienced in the war. I had hidden the pages in the dining-room sideboard. One day I found the children reading them. Hilary (12), Bernice (7) and Harris (6) were sitting together on the settee crying their eyes out. They knew that I had been in different camps, but I had deliberately spared them the details.

They were very upset that I hadn't told them before but I had been worried that such information might affect their health, and so we kept off the subject. Norman had to concentrate on making a living, and I wanted to forget the past. Even our closest friends never realised exactly what I had been through.

With hindsight, maybe I should have told them earlier, but I wanted them to reach a certain age so that they would have a better, more mature understanding of the situation.

The children were sympathetic, not angry. They simply wanted to know the facts, the true picture, but they soon saw that talking about it distressed me too much and so they stopped asking me questions.

Now, they are all grown-up and they fully understand. They are not bitter and appreciate the reasons for my reticence at that time. My own grandchildren are keen for me to talk to their schools. Norman and I do quite a lot of public speaking to organisations (Jewish and non-Jewish) all over the country and abroad: in Holland, France, Germany, Canada. One question I keep being asked is: 'Why did I not try to escape?' People cannot grasp why we did not fight back. But how could we retaliate? With our bare hands? To whom could we turn? We were helpless people, so how could we rebel? We had no weapons, no means of defending ourselves. Wherever we walked we were guarded by the SS and by Alsatian dogs. The Nazis always had a way of dragging a person back and those who tried to escape were so severely punished that it just wasn't worth the risk.

I feel very privileged today to be able to write and speak about the things that happened to me because, however painful it is for me, I think it is vitally important for the younger generation to know the truth. Because that period of history is central to my life, I feel that I must make people aware of the truth, so that such atrocities may never be contemplated again.

I believe that the rise of Fascism in Germany in the thirties and the events to which this led should be an essential part of the syllabus in every school in Britain. It is too easy for young people today to be influenced by evil elements in society. Young fellows may think it's fun to flaunt Fascist salutes or to wear Hitler sweatshirts, but such tactics are dangerous and can persuade impressionable young people to adopt this evil way of thinking.

If schools and universities were to incorporate teaching about Nazi Germany into their curricula, they would be helping to promote an atmosphere of greater understanding and mutual respect. Someone who has suffered from hunger will always understand another who is hungry, but a person who is well fed can never perceive what it is like to be hungry.

Whenever I see a German man of about seventy, I put a uniform on him. I can tell by his looks that he might have been a high-ranking Nazi official and I wonder: 'How many people has he got on his conscience?' I do not feel sorry for him, in the sense that maybe he didn't know what he was doing. He did know. I feel resentment and hurt, and I remind myself that my people lost their lives for no reason, for no crime committed, for nothing.

I enjoy helping Norman in the business and accompanying him abroad on business trips. We occasionally go to Frankfurt, but I try to separate my feelings about the past on such occasions. I try to be tolerant, but always at the back of my mind I wonder what the older German men I see were doing during the war.

Much as I would love to cut myself off from that part of my life, it is impossible.

Being occupied with bringing up children and working with various charities (like the Ethiopian famine campaign or Alexandra Rose Day) has helped me to forget. I would recommend anybody to find some sort of positive, therapeutic outlet – for instance, sport, charity work, writing, reading – in order to be able to express themselves. For myself, I find that reading can make me depressed as I tend to relate certain books and themes to my past. I prefer to become involved in less introspective pursuits. Helping people who are in need or despair means a lot to me.

Subconsciously perhaps, I make comparisons between my life now and in the war years. It irritates me to hear people being petty. There are so many more important issues in the world than arguing over trivialities.

I hope and pray that the young of today will try to live in harmony with other races, religions and creeds and that there will be a better tomorrow for the generations to come.

11

I Light a Candle

Rabbi Leslie Hardman, who married us at Lübeck, said during a television interview* forty years later that after burying about thirty thousand people in April 1945 he finally heard the word 'love'. He saw our wedding as a symbol of life after death.

It was 1985, we were approaching our fortieth wedding anniversary, and I said to Norman one day: 'Wouldn't it be nice if we could go back to Belsen, where we met?' I knew this was bound to stir up old memories but I felt it was important to remember the past and the circumstances of our first meeting.

The following day the British Legion rang us with information about the coming fortieth anniversary celebrations of the liberation of Belsen. Soon afterwards we received invitations to visit Belsen, first from the Westphalia area authority, and then from a German TV company.

I contacted Rabbi Hardman and suggested that he come with us, but unfortunately he was unable to make it as he had to go to America.

Next, I had John Knight of the *Sunday Mirror* on the line, then Breakfast Television, then BBC Television's 'The Time of Your Life' programme. The news of our proposed visit to Belsen spread so fast that our telephone hardly stopped ringing, with all

* Noel Edmonds' 'The Time of Your Life' programme on BBC TV shown in July 1985.

the top reporters and photographers chasing us for a story, preferably an 'exclusive'.

Finally, a German television company paid for our flight, and also lunch the following day. We were met at Hanover airport by a woman TV journalist, and we all stayed overnight in a hotel, in the town. It was two o'clock the following morning before we got to bed, because she became so involved and fascinated with questioning us that she could not tear herself away.

The following morning the TV people came to collect us in a car with a camera and other equipment, and drove us to Belsen. The journey was about thirty miles, through a thickly wooded area which I remembered well from forty years ago. I tried to control my emotions but the tears were running down my face.

I could still hear the voices of the guards shouting *"Raus! 'Raus!"* when the train stopped in the middle of the woods. It was like an echo in the head.

On the way there, I bought some tulips and carnations to place on the mass graves.

When we arrived at Belsen gate, Michael Cole of BBC television news was waiting with the crew. The German reporter was annoyed since she thought that her company had exclusive coverage of our story. She said to me: 'When we get to the memorial park, please remember to speak in German.'

Michael Cole came over and introduced himself. I asked him how he knew who we were. He said: 'Oh, I have all the details. Would you please give us some of your time?'

I suggested that they sort it out between themselves. He couldn't speak German, but she spoke some English. She said: 'We want them first. We brought them over here' – and so on.

I said: 'Let's not quarrel. We'll give you *both* time.'

We all walked through the gates into the camp, Michael Cole and his crew carrying microphones and other equipment. I started talking in English and the German reporter turned round sharply and said: 'Please speak in German.'

Eventually, the German TV people took me on one side and

interviewed me live. Afterwards, Norman and I did a separate interview for Michael Cole and BBC television news. The crew spent the whole day with us, filming us as we walked around the memorial park.

At four o'clock the German crew left, and then we were joined by Wendy Sturgess, producer of BBC Television's 'The Time of Your Life' series, and the programme's presenter Noel Edmonds.

We were at the media's beck and call non-stop from eight a.m. until eight p.m. I was completely exhausted. Back at the hotel I could not sleep, because it had all been such an overwhelming experience. So many thoughts and memories had gone rushing through my mind, as I walked on the soil where I had walked forty years before with my boots, my sorrows. Everything looks so beautiful now, and yet so clinical. The grass is not like real grass. It looks coarse, dull, artificial. None of the original buildings remain.

What I was really seeing was not the neat grass or the well-ordered park. I had to make my own picture, the way it once was: the gates where I entered and saw on the right the hospital barrack, and on the left the living quarters of the women SS, and in the centre a pond full of muddy water. Walk on a bit further and you would come to another set of barracks, the *Komman-dantur*, where the British Army made their headquarters when they liberated Belsen. Further on again were the inmates' barracks.

I remembered Irma Grese and her cronies counting and searching us at the hospital gate, where on my first day as a nurse Irma Grese lashed my cheek and stole my sister's photograph.

I think a permanent reminder of the camp should have been left there: one of the original barracks, perhaps – because most people today have no idea what the place actually looked like. It is very quiet, like a cemetery, but there is such a *cry* there, a cry buried with the tears, the talents, the emotions. When you tread on the grass you can feel the despair of generations who, in the normal way, could have contributed so much to their society.

We met a group of German rockers dressed in black leather jackets and trousers, and riding their motor cycles. They wanted to speak to me and to know the truth. I asked them why they were so interested. They said they wanted to know the facts from me at first-hand, because their grandparents never talked about the war and their parents said it was all propaganda.

After listening to me, these young people said they believed what I had told them, and they would spread the word among their friends that it really was true and that their parents' and grandparents' version of events was a big lie.

And as I looked at them I could see the tears rolling down their cheeks. I was amazed, and very moved. I felt a sense of regeneration, of renewal, a sense that they wanted to make a difference to society.

So, although it is painful for me to remind myself about that period in my life, I feel that my children and grandchildren will live a better, more harmonious youth than I did, because I spent the best years of my life in a concentration camp.

We also met a group of about thirty gypsies, who came with their leader. We passed them as they were entering the camp and we were going out to have lunch. They seemed very angry. I wondered what the matter was and why they were shouting so aggressively. Apparently they had wanted to make a speech and to take part in the television broadcast when Chancellor Kohl was there, but they had been told they were not allowed to appear because they were gypsies.

I said: 'Look – don't argue. Just thank God you are alive. So . . . you are not appearing on the programme? You can still come and listen to other people. And you can bring flowers.'

I felt sorry that they were being denied the opportunity to put their case. After all, 35,000 of them died in the camps. I had not come across any of them at Plaszov, Auschwitz or Belsen but, like other minority groups (such as political prisoners), they would have been based in separate areas within the camps. I asked the German reporter: 'Why can't they speak on the programme?'

'Oh, political reasons,' she replied. She did not elaborate, but it was clearly a case of discrimination.

It was so stupid and unjust. They had suffered just as much as the rest of us. They, too, had lost members of their families in the Holocaust.

We met them again later at a restaurant in the village outside the camp. The whole group was sitting at a table in the corner, and one of them came over and apologised for his behaviour, saying that it was nothing personal against me. So we parted friends.

On Saturday we went to the synagogue, and some people we met there had seen us on German TV. They kept coming and shaking our hands, saying: 'Thank you. You've done so much good.'

On Sunday morning the actual memorial service took place. It was a beautiful day, chilly but sunny, and well over a thousand people had come to pay their respects from all over the world. Roughly 20 per cent were survivors. Chancellor Helmut Kohl made a speech.

Afterwards we were invited to a reception in one of the halls, where we were introduced to the British consul, the president of the Jewish community and other top people. There was no one there whom I could be absolutely sure I knew from the camps. Forty years is a long time, but one woman came over to me and said she recognised my voice and was happy to see me again. She gave me her card and if I go to Germany again, I will visit her. She lives in Hanover.

A surprising number of survivors live in Germany. I cannot understand how they can bear to settle there after all they went through in the war. One Jewish couple I met lived not far from Belsen. I would love to have asked them why, but they might have told me to mind my own business!

I suppose they have made a life for themselves there. Personally, I could never have done that because all the time I would have felt I was living in a glorified, extended camp. Those times, that

I wanted so much to put behind me, would have been too close to me there.

I was sorry that none of my children could be present, because it was interesting to see the children of the survivors and to notice how moved they were by the occasion. Our son and daughters watched us on television and they cried, all three of them. They had tried to persuade me not to go, because they felt it would be too much for me emotionally.

I did have doubts about whether I would be able to cope. I prayed for the strength to get me through this reunion and back to my daily routine in England, and to let the memories fade, but this is difficult. If I can remember all the details after forty years, it shows you how fresh everything is in my mind.

Norman wasn't very keen at first on my returning to Belsen, in case I found it too traumatic, but I wanted to go back, to show that I hadn't forgotten about the people who lost their lives there. How many families – whole generations – must have been destroyed, with no one left to offer a flower or say a prayer on their behalf?

I feel emotional about my past. When I meet some people who have been through the Holocaust, they seem to have got so hard. They 'shut off' from their experiences too much, and I don't believe it does them any good. They should let their emotions out more.

Everyone reacts in different ways, but in my own case going back to Belsen made me appreciate once again the fact that I am alive today and able to make a tiny contribution to the memory of those who died there. I went to give a prayer and offer a flower, because I knew the people and this is one way of maintaining the contact, the link between us.

There are signposts and arrows outside the camp marked 'Bergen-Belsen' for the benefit of tourists. The local inhabitants still deny they knew a concentration camp existed in their district. I find this hard to believe. I can understand that they were frightened, but why still pretend not to have known the truth?

It is good that people want to go to Belsen and see for themselves the scene of the Nazis' crimes. There are regular school outings there in Germany and I observed a party of young girls and boys looking with great interest at papers and documents in the little museum at Belsen. I am sure that some of them carry the guilt and shame that such outrages could take place in their own country.

Hopefully, their generation will learn from the mistakes their parents and grandparents made, and will adopt a different, more humane way of life. People should not be afraid of one another, as we were.

The following month, May 1985, we attended a memorial service in Hyde Park, London, for Jewish ex-servicemen. Hundreds of people attended from almost every unit in the Army, and once again Norman and I were besieged by the press. It was a cold day and I was feeling so choked that I couldn't say much at first. When I had calmed down a little, I answered more questions. The cameras clicked away and the following morning our photo-graph was splashed all over the front pages. It was like history repeating itself.

I was surprised and moved at the continuing interest in our story. I had thought it would fade away, but everyone recognised us and several days later the papers were still writing about us.

People brought flowers and wreaths to lay on the memorial, but for me the occasion had not got the same meaning as Belsen. I wasn't listening to the speeches (by the Chief Rabbi, Greville Janner MP and others), because I had my own story and I mourned in my own way.

Every autumn, at Yom Kippur, we light candles and they burn all day and night in memory of the people we have lost. I know that when I light a candle in memory of my sisters and brothers, that is my own personal tribute. I don't have to talk about it and people don't need to remind me about it, because I can never forget.

Norman, too, saw only the original picture of Belsen camp, a wasteland without trees, flowers or grass. He still saw the walking skeletons, still felt the air of death about the place. Like his fellow soldiers who came to liberate us, he always has that picture of a living hell in front of him, and not the neat-looking memorial park of today.

Epilogue

---

by Norman Turgel

For anyone who went through a period in the concentration camps, whether it was six months or six years, the effect on the human brain must have been appalling. From what I have seen of most survivors, they still feel haunted or 'locked away'. They still have a constant inner fear.

Our GP, Dr Herbert Julian Davies, has known Gena since he first came to Edgware in 1960, and he has always been impressed by her powerful personality and the courageous way in which she has dealt with many of the problems relating to her past.

He believes, as I do, that Gena is highly determined and mentally strong. On the other hand, if she has an ache or pain, or some physical symptom, this tends to be magnified out of all proportion because of that sense of lingering terror that lies deeply buried in survivors, making them unable to differentiate between a minor symptom and a major one.

In his long experience of treating Holocaust survivors, Dr Davies has found that, between the ages of forty and sixty, all the traumas which they have previously suppressed tend to reappear in various ways. They may feel depressed or isolated. They are prey to physical or psychosomatic illnesses. They are never a hundred per cent relaxed. There is always a neurotic feeling about them. One senses that they are walking a narrow pathway of sanity and that there is a sort of nightmarish quality about their voices.

He says he can spot them as soon as they come into the room. He can see that they have been through an experience and that it hasn't necessarily been ennobling. They are all scarred in some way. We both agree that people who have lived through this kind of experience tend to fall into one of two categories: they either give way completely or else, like Gena, become tremendous personalities with boundless energy. This may be a way of getting rid of their guilt at survival. They have this power, the need to show or prove something to the people they have left behind.

Mrs Goldfinger, Gena's mother, was also a remarkable personality whom Dr Davies came to know well. He is convinced that she only survived and was able to cope because of the love, care and devotion that Gena gave to her. To have survived, after seeing what happened to her other children, and still come through it with a sense of humour and a fund of stories, was a marvellous tribute to the strength of character of both mother and daughter. She loved to be the centre of attention, and she could talk for hours about life in Eastern Europe and Poland. She was generous and kind to her relatives, but she was the boss and she could of course be difficult at times.

Because of her agoraphobia, her hairdresser came to the house at least once a week. We could never leave her for long – a few days at the most. We had few holidays, as we always had to have somebody at home to be with her.

Gena and I have not spent a day without seeing each other since the day we were married. When I go away on business, she comes with me. She travels with me all over the world, to Hong Kong, Canada, Holland, America ... It just seems natural. I don't like to leave her on her own. I have always felt that I must be with her, and I know she feels that way too. She's a part of me, and I'm part of her.

Once, when our son Harris was about ten years old, I flew to France in the morning, and I was back again by the end of the afternoon. I phoned her from Paris on my arrival and said I was getting the next flight back and never again would I go away on my own. I was supposed to stay there two days, but I was missing her and would have been worried about leaving her on her own for longer.

There were many nights, early in our marriage, when I woke up to find her screaming, after a nightmare, and had to quieten her. But I got used to it and I knew when I married her that there would be certain times when I would have to take special care of her. But she is certainly worth it. She has a fantastic character and has never complained about anything. Even in her not-such-good-health she will still think of others and try to help them.

She does a lot of charity work, which she finds fulfilling, especially if it is connected with children, as she has seen her own nephews and nieces – in Poland and the camps – being killed for no reason. On our ruby wedding anniversary in 1985, we gave an oxygen analyser to the Baby Unit at Edgware General Hospital, and we both do a stint at the hospital on Christmas Day, to give the nurses a break.

We have never been parted for more than a few hours at a time. The only such occasions were when she was in hospital for the birth of our children, and similarly, when I was in hospital for a minor operation a few years ago. At night we had to arrange for one of the children to stay with her.

We think alike. Sometimes I will say something and she asks me: 'How did you know I was thinking about that?' We are very close, and the extraordinary, unique way in which we met has strengthened our bond, though I was always sure that we would make a success of our married life. When we were first married, we had difficult times, but somehow it didn't matter. We had very little in material terms, but we had children and we looked after them. Having a family early on took her mind off the traumatic things that had happened to her during the war years.

I ring her as soon as I arrive at the office, and several times during the day as well. If I don't phone by 10 a.m. I get a call: 'What's the matter? Aren't you talking to me today?'

Unlike some survivors, Gena has come to terms with herself. She made up her mind from the beginning that she was going to live a new life and to absorb English culture, and she has adjusted remarkably well. She is now reaping the rewards of the life that she made for herself in England.

When she sees a new generation of Germans, she realises that the Holocaust was before their time, but when she sees people over the age of sixty or so she feels that these are the people who could have been her oppressors.

If I meet any German person in that age bracket, I find myself wondering: 'What did this man or woman do during the war?'

When one recalls the pictures of thousands of men, women and children in Nazi Germany chanting '*Sieg Heil!*' and '*Heil Führer!*' one feels that all the people one meets above a certain age must have been Nazis and known what was going on. That situation has not arisen much in our business, as we deal mainly with younger people. However, it was only a few years ago that I myself felt inclined to start doing business in Germany at all.

About ten years ago a German in his early forties came into our office and wanted to buy some goods direct from us instead of through an agent. I told him we didn't sell to Germany and I explained my reasons. He assured me that his family had never been Nazis, and later he produced a letter from his local Jewish organisation which stated that his father had helped Jewish people and that his family were not National Socialists. Since then we have carried on doing business together, as I feel that people below fifty could not have committed any of the crimes which the SS were capable of doing.

How a country which was supposed to have been so civilised – a country which produced composers like Wagner and Bach, authors like Goethe – could have sunk to such a low level of brutality, I will never understand.

Like Gena, I believe that there should be much more emphasis on history in Britain's schools, for the benefit of the younger generation. In Germany they teach their children what happened in the Holocaust. The new generation of Germans still feel they bear the guilt of their parents and grandparents, which won't be erased for some generations to come. Then it will pass into history.

It must live on, in books and stories like Gena's. It must never be forgotten. The new generation should never forget what happened when civilisation sank to its lowest depth. Gena has tried to forgive, but she can never forget.